# HISTORIC DISASTERS
# OF NEW ENGLAND

# HISTORIC DISASTERS OF NEW ENGLAND

## Legendary Storms, Twisters, Floods, and Other Catastrophes

### RANDI MINETOR

Down East Books

Camden, Maine

# Down East Books

Published by Down East Books
An imprint of The Rowman & Littlefield Publishing Group, Inc.
4501 Forbes Blvd., Suite 200
Lanham, MD 20706
www.rowman.com

Distributed by NATIONAL BOOK NETWORK

British Library Cataloguing in Publication Information Available

**Library of Congress Cataloging-in-Publication Data**
Names: Minetor, Randi, author.
Title: Historic disasters of New England : legendary storms, twisters, floods, and other catastrophes / Randi Minetor.
Description: Camden, Maine ; Lanham, Maryland : Down East Books, [2021] | "Distributed by NATIONAL BOOK NETWORK"—T.p. verso. | Includes bibliographical references. | Summary: "Historic Disasters of New England tells the stories of the biggest and baddest natural calamities to have struck the region, including: The 4-state tornado swarm of 1787 The October Gale 1841 The Great Blizzard of 1888 The Heat Wave of 1911 The Twin Hurricanes of 1954 And lots more"— Provided by publisher.
Identifiers: LCCN 2020052112 (print) | LCCN 2020052113 (ebook) | ISBN 9781608937134 (Paperback : alk. paper) | ISBN 9781608937394 (ePub)
Subjects: LCSH: Natural disasters—New England—History.
Classification: LCC GB5010 .M56 2021 (print) | LCC GB5010 (ebook) | DDC 904/.5—dc23
LC record available at https://lccn.loc.gov/2020052112
LC ebook record available at https://lccn.loc.gov/2020052113

♾️™ The paper used in this publication meets the minimum requirements of American National Standard for Information Sciences—Permanence of Paper for Printed Library Materials, ANSI/NISO Z39.48-1992.

# Contents

# Introduction
## The Night Vermont Flooded

When Nic and I posted on Facebook in late August 2011 about our plans to spend the weekend in Vermont, friends across the country responded with alarm.

"Don't go," a high school friend living in San Diego pleaded. "You've seen the forecast, right?" Another said, "If you get stuck there, I get to say 'I told you so.'"

The forecast of another "storm of the century" seemed—pardon the pun—significantly overblown. A Category 1 hurricane called Irene had taken a turn northward up the East Coast, looking as if it might make landfall in the Carolinas on Saturday, August 27, the second day of our three-day weekend trip. Our plans in Grafton and Weston could hardly be affected by weather in North Carolina, we thought, and even if the storm did continue northward into Long Island Sound, we had no plans to approach New England's southern coast. Landlocked central Vermont, we reasoned, had to be one of the least hurricane-prone areas in the Northeast.

We arrived at the home of our friends Bil Walters and Christine Tattersall in Houghtonville, Vermont, late in the day on Friday, August 26, for a weekend house party of food, drink, and theater at the Weston Playhouse. Our friends Ken Horowitz, Rose-Anne Moore, and Bruce Barton were part of the festivities as well, joining us from Connecticut and New York City. We planned nothing more strenuous than grilling steaks and cleaning out Bil's collection of peculiar, and sometimes unpalatable liqueurs, and waiting out what forecasters said would be a heavy rain of about three inches on Saturday night.

Right on schedule, the upper edge of Irene arrived, and rain began on Saturday as we made our way back to the house after the performance. The shower fell quietly but steadily, hard enough that I chose

1

to skip filling our Subaru Outback's nearly empty tank at the only gas station on our route between Weston and Houghtonville.

We arrived back at the Walters' home and settled in around the dining room table. I made a quick Facebook post to let our friends far and wide know that we were just fine: "We are back and enjoying a lovely selection of liqueurs, and listening to the gentle rain." There we were in the photo, seven of us, raising our glasses and grinning into the lens, knowing for certain that our silly friends across the country had been concerned about us for nothing. We sipped Benedictine and syrupy cherry Grand Marnier and turned in around midnight, planning on brunch and a long drive home in the morning.

I awoke in darkness sometime later, startled out of a dream by a sound that reminded me of a bowling ball hitting the pins and scoring a strike. As I gained full consciousness, I understood that rain pounded the roof, hammering so loudly that I could barely distinguish other sounds beyond it. There it was again, though—clacking, bonking, rolling, then coming to a stop before starting over again with an otherworldly arrhythmia. I tried to make sense of it, but soon the regular roar of the downpour lulled me back into relaxation. Whatever it was would have to wait to be deciphered until morning.

When I opened my eyes again sometime later, the room contained the light of a cold dawn. Nic stood wrapped in his robe, looking out the bedroom window. "What?" I said.

"The road is a river," he replied. "And we're an island."

I joined him at the window. The river that flowed several hundred feet away from the house had somehow rerouted into the road, and it ran deep enough and swiftly enough to create its own rapids. In a moment I heard the undecipherable sound again and saw what made it: boulders rolling down the riverbed, pushed by what could only be described as pounding surf. Rocks from higher up in the mountains came tumbling down with the swollen river waters, pushed ahead by other debris, and propelled to the bottom of the riverbed. They formed an impromptu dam, piling up and diverting the river into the road and beyond, and flooding the Walters' yard. The grassy expanse swirled with a rapid current.

Lucky for us, the century-old house stood on a slight rise, giving it just enough height above the water to keep it comparatively dry as the wide side yard and all the land between us and the neighbors vanished under a widening milky-beige pool. As the rain continued to spatter its surface, the water shook and shimmered, and we watched as the down-spouts from all the houses in sight poured a steady pulse of rainwater into the repositioned river.

We dressed in a hurry and headed downstairs where the rest of our party clustered around the radio in the kitchen. Reports came in from all over Vermont about roads washed out, bridges swept away by floodwaters pouring down from the Green Mountains, and build-ings filling with water as rivers and streams crested their banks. More than seven thousand miles of rivers crisscrossed the state, and as eleven inches of rain filled waterways already saturated from a rainy summer, just about every one of them overflowed. Route 4, our road home-ward, had been decimated by flood damage. Several of the state's his-toric covered bridges crumbled in the path of flood debris gathered by rushing waters—walls of branches, silt, mud, and parts of other bridges careening down mountainsides and crashing through anything in their path.

One report stood out for us: the Weston Playhouse, where we had enjoyed a performance just hours before, stood in the middle of the flooded Weston town square, its newly completed infrastructure reno-vations ruined.

Connecticut, where Hurricane Irene had lashed the coastline with wind as well as torrential rain, reported that 754,000 homes were with-out electrical power—a number that represented the entire eastern half of the state. Two people there died in fires set off by downed power lines, and a third drowned when his canoe turned over and dumped him into rising waters. In East Haven, twenty homes were destroyed along the coast of the Long Island Sound. Overall, however, the state escaped widespread devastation, good news for Ken and Rose-Anne, whose home is just behind one of Connecticut's coastal seawalls. Massachu-setts had seen the kind of flooding we witnessed now—two rivers, the Westfield and the Deerfield, had crested their banks at levels not seen since the Great New England Hurricane of 1938. Nearly every resident of Rhode Island lost power as seventy-mile-per-hour winds knocked down trees and power lines, but the hurricane barrier in Providence held up against the storm surge from Narragansett Bay, sparing the city the kind of flooding it had seen in 1938 and 1954.

We breathed a sigh of relief that the wind had not moved up into Vermont, but even without this added hazard, our troubles had only begun. The rising waters around us crept up the incline on their way to Bil and Christine's basement.

In a moment of stunningly clearheaded thinking, Nic—the son of a machinist, and a superhero with a toolbelt—headed down into the earthen basement to check on the functioning of the sump pump. He found that Bil had recently installed a new one, but it would not be enough to handle the water already seeping into the underground room—so he pressed the old one into service as well, jerry-rigging a mechanism that doubled the pumping power. The Walters' house was saved for the time being, but Bil and Christine were the only year-round residents in this cluster of homes, and the other houses must surely already have high water in their basements. Christine pulled on boots and made her way through the knee-deep water to peer into cellar windows, gesturing her findings to the rest of us as we stood on her porch and watched, marveling at the road that became a river.

We behaved as if we had all been knocked out of the normal time-stream, neglecting the usual house party activities of Sunday brunch, and packing our cases. We listened to the news reports on the radio, waved down any Vermonters who sloshed their way up the road on foot in hopes of reaching Grafton—another four miles east—and kept an eye on the basement pumping rig, which managed to keep the house free from flooding even as the waters rose higher. At 7:30 p.m., as we sat around the table eating pasta with home-grown basil pesto Christine had liberated from the freezer, the lights flickered and went out. Christine brought out candles as Bil reminded us that the house's water supply came from a well—so with no power, the well's pump wouldn't work. We exchanged uneasy glances as we faced a night without clean water or working toilets.

On Monday morning, however, electrical power had come back online, and the rain had finally stopped. We learned that Hurricane Irene, despite being downgraded to a tropical storm by the time it reached Vermont, had done far more damage in the state than we could have imagined. The total required for rebuilding roads and bridges, redirecting rivers back into their banks, and repairing or replacing damaged buildings ran as high as $733 million, only a fraction of which would come from federal emergency management funds. Vermont had a long rebuild ahead of it, not the least of which would involve the construction of safeguards to help mitigate the effects of the next major storm, whenever that might arrive.

It took us most of the day Monday to make our way out of Houghtonville, secure a tank of gas (getting trapped in a disaster area with an empty gas tank is a mistake I will never make again), and begin the crawl back to New York State. Crossing the state line brought no relief, however: We found that Irene had left parts of the lower Hudson River valley in ruins as well, suspending commuter train activity and making it nearly impossible for Bruce to get back to his apartment in New Jersey. We finally left him at the Poughkeepsie station shortly after dark, where he was assured that a train would take him into New York City eventually. It was 3:00 a.m., however, before he saw his own bed.

Irene was only the second tropical storm in Vermont's history to make actual landfall in the state, and scientists, including Kerry Emanuel, professor of atmospheric science at the Massachusetts Institute of Technology, said that Irene was a "thousand-year storm," the kind of storm that only comes once in a millennium. That label, however, is based on twentieth-century data. In the age of rapidly advancing climate change, storms like Irene are no longer the outliers they once were. "At the end of this century, if we do nothing to curb emissions, that 1,000-year event in rain would be a 100-year event," Emanuel told the website InsideClimate News in 2016.

Seeing a New England hurricane firsthand—even a downgraded one—brought into sharp relief the weather's ability to transform a landscape in a matter of hours. I knew, however, that while we had had a close call, many New Englanders throughout recorded history have faced far fiercer threats from natural forces, and some did not survive the experience.

This book is not like the six books I've written in the "Death in the Parks" series; I make no attempt here to supply an exhaustive list of the many deaths that have occurred during hurricanes, tornadoes, fires, floods, and one bizarre accident with a molasses tank. Instead, *Historic Disasters of New England* tells selected stories of the perils these events present, the people who found themselves in danger, and the astounding resiliency New Englanders demonstrate in the face of chaos—especially those on the southern and eastern coasts.

The good news is that weather forecasting, mass communication, and mitigation technology have all advanced exponentially since the early storms and other disasters described in this book, so the loss of power, property, and life have diminished over the last several decades. The most dramatic stories are those of the days before all of these modern prediction tools—the ones that came upon New Englanders with little or no warning. While storms have become much more frequent and more severe in recent years, as if compensating for humans' ability to withstand the impact, I chose to look at historic events that demonstrate the resiliency of America's most northeastern residents. New Englanders have survived all manner of emergencies and catastrophic weather, even when they had little more than axes and shovel with which to rebuild. Perhaps this gives us hope for surviving the more frequent and violent storms arriving with the acceleration of climate change.

This being said, if I have skipped over your favorite natural disasters in favor of others that may be slightly more legendary, I humbly apologize. I hope that enough people will enjoy this book that a second volume will be warranted, in which I can explore more of nature's demonstrations of wrath in New England throughout the nineteenth, twentieth, and twenty-first centuries.

Join me in exploring the perils of seacoast life, the dangers lurking in the forests, and the threats found along rivers and streams throughout Connecticut, Maine, Massachusetts, New Hampshire, Rhode Island, and Vermont. Marvel with me at the fact that you have not yet succumbed, when so many hazards come to visit you in your own backyard.

## CHAPTER ONE

# "'Tis Never Good For Man Nor Beast"— The Storm of 1635

Hard as it is to believe in an age of instant answers to every question, people once lived in a time when they could not obtain a scientifically prepared, reasonably accurate weather forecast. Weather predictions did not appear in the mass media—that is, in newspapers—until the Smithsonian Institution, the central repository of the nation's scientific information, became the nucleus of a new system of weather-information gathering in 1860.

Early that year, the Washington, DC, *Evening Star* suggested to its readers that just looking at the sky could indicate weather. "The colors of the sky at particular times afford wonderfully good guidance," it noted. "Not only does a rosy sunset presage fair weather, and a ruddy sunrise bad weather, but there are other tints which speak with equal clearness and accuracy. A bright yellow sky in the evening indicates wind; a pale yellow, wet; a neutral grey color constitutes a favorable sign in the evening, an unfavorable one in the morning. . . . These are simple maxims; and yet not so simple but that the English Board of Trade has thought fit to publish them for the use of seafaring men."

Remarkably, just twenty days earlier on January 6, 1860, the *Evening Star* published its first real weather report—in fact, the first one in American history. It carried the observations made across the country and transmitted over the American Consolidated Telegraph Line, which led to a bank of learned men within the Smithsonian. Stations from New York City in the north to New Orleans, Louisiana, in the south and west provided their weather observations in the simplest terms: "clear, cold," noted New York, while Norfolk, Virginia, added the temperature (16 degrees, presumably Fahrenheit) and the wind direction (NW). The information from the twenty-eight reporting weather stations allowed Smithsonian scientists to begin to understand weather patterns, peeling away the first layer of mystery and creating a new science of meteorology.

Barely a year later, the Civil War ended communication with the southern states and curtailed the growth of the new weather network, but the foundation of weather forecasting had been laid, and science would push forward once again later in the century when connections could be reestablished.

These firsts in weather observation and prediction came more than two centuries too late for the earliest European settlers in New England's colonies, however. For residents of Jamestown, Virginia, and Plimouth Plantation in what would become Massachusetts, the brewing of a major storm might only become apparent when the wind began to pick up speed and force as it reached the coastline, either moving in from the east over the Atlantic Ocean, or from the west or north over the vast forests. "When the wind is out of the East, 'tis never good for man nor beast," an old proverb warned, and the violent gales that often followed made good on the saying's promise.

How did these colonists of the 1600s determine if they were in the path of a storm at any time of year? Nearly one hundred years before the invention of the thermometer and at least a decade before the first barometer measured changes in atmospheric pressure, they had to rely on their eyes, ears, and the knowledge—more to the point, superstitions—passed down by their elders.

Perhaps they observed their cattle gaining heavy wooly coats as the warm summer days ended and the trees near Plimouth Plantation began turning auburn and scarlet. Cows and sheep with thicker than normal coats—a subjective judgment in the best of times—might indicate a particularly cold and snowy winter on its way, as good a sign as any that the colonists needed to chop extra firewood and seal the cracks in their homes against freezing temperatures. As a storm approached, cattle may have bunched together in a corner of a pen or farmyard, a defensive posture against wind and rain that may have served as a warning to their human caretakers.

In this Currier & Ives representation, the Pilgrims landed at what would become Plymouth Colony. (Courtesy Library of Congress)

If the rabbits and squirrels in the nearby forests looked especially fat, they might be taking on extra insulation for an unusually frigid season as well. Perhaps settlers busy with housekeeping tasks noted more mice than usual attempting to make themselves at home inside their human neighbors' buildings, or spiders constructing uncommonly large webs to catch extra food. Moles digging particularly deep holes—reported as more than 2.5 feet—may have indicated that they felt a very cold season coming on. Any of these signs might have made colonists believe that storms or blizzards approached, even if the animals appeared to sense events that were still several months off.

Members of the new colonies may have seen the change of seasons enough times during their early years in Plimouth to note when trees that bore fruit or nuts produced particularly abundant crops, providing the additional food animals needed for a harsher than normal winter ahead. Even before the season changed, colonists may have looked at the moon as it rose in the night sky and noted a ring around it, the most dependable warning that rain or snow would arrive in a day or so.

All these signs might mean nothing at all, of course, but these were the best means the colonists had of guessing what kind of weather might be on its way in the near term. Amid these old wives' tales and suppositions, one sign actually provided real evidence: an eastern sky glowing red in the early morning. Colonist William Bradford and other seasoned sailors knew exactly what this foretold: the sun dyeing heavy, wet clouds in shades of salmon and coral, a sure indication of a storm crossing the ocean on its way to the colony.

Bradford did history the courtesy of writing a careful record of Plimouth's early days, providing us with the only evidence of a massive storm that rocked the colony in 1635. "This year, y' 14. or 15. of August [being Saturday] was such a mighty storme of wind & raine, as none living in thee parts, either English or Indeans, ever saw," he wrote. "Being like [for y' time it continued] to those Hauricanes and Tuffons that writers make mention of in y' Indeas. It began in y' morning, a litle before day, and grue not by degrees, but came with violence in y' begining, to y' great amasemente of many."

Bradford's archaic language and abysmal spelling notwithstanding, the gale certainly seemed cataclysmic to the colonists, blowing down a total of 211 houses and tearing the roofs off others. He reported that the storm caused a number of ships to be lost at sea and placed others in "extreme danger," swelling the sea's waves to twenty feet "right up & downe" in height. Native tribesmen and their families climbed trees to escape the waves, but this may have been exactly the wrong strategy. The winds caused "many hundered thowsands of trees" to topple, the largest of them yanked out of the ground by their roots and the tops of the tallest pine trees seared off. Bradford saw "tall yonge oaks & walnut trees . . . wound like a withe," twisted by the wind and "very strang & fearfull to behould."

The terrible storm continued for five or six hours, Bradford said, coming at the colony from the southeast and splitting itself into several parts, finally abating and making its way back to the south and east. "The signes and marks of it will remaine this 100. years in these parts wher it was sorest," he completed his account. In a last note, he added, "The moons suffered a great eclips the 2. night after it."

Further descriptions come from the journal of John Winthrop, then governor of the Massachusetts Bay Colony. "The wind having blown hard at S. and S.W. a week before, about midnight it came up at N.E. and blew with such violence, with abundance of rain, that it blew down many hundreds of trees, near the towns, overthrew some houses [and] drave the ships from their anchors," he wrote. He made special note of a ship called the *Great Hope*, a four hundred-ton ocean vessel from Ipswich, which the wind drove aground at Mr. Hoff's Point (the location is no more specific than that, but historians believe it was near Charlestown). When the wind changed direction and came at the ship again from the northwest, it blew hard enough to free the ship from its position and take it out into the bay. The gale carried the *Great Hope* all the way to Charlestown, on the Atlantic shore in modern-day Boston . . . and ran it aground again there.

Winthrop also described a phenomenon he called a "double tide." At about 8:00 p.m., he said the wind came at the coastline "very strong and, it being then about high water, by nine the tide was fallen about three feet." Barely an hour later, it had risen once again by two or three feet, "which was conceived to be, that the sea was grown so high abroad with the N.E. wind, that, meeting with the ebb, it forced it back again." We can only imagine what kind of havoc the eventual high tide caused, as Winthrop doesn't describe it, but he does note that the double tide extended well to the south, where the storm was "more violent."

He tells the story of the *James*, a ship out of Bristol, England, carrying "one hundred passengers, honest people of Yorkshire." The *James*, with Captain John Taylor at the helm, left England on June 3 and finally cleared English waters on June 22, accompanied by four ships— the *Elizabeth*, the *Mary*, and the *Diligence*—headed for Newfoundland, and the *Angel Gabriel*, a well-armed merchant ship with guns so large they limited its ability to carry many passengers. The *Gabriel* was packed with enough provisions for the people on board—about thirty would-be colonists on their way to the New World, and an untold number of crew members—for a twelve-week voyage. It also carried cattle and all the furnishings and trunks required for the passengers to begin their new lives.

The *James* and *Angel Gabriel* traveled relatively close to one another across the Atlantic's deep waters, with the lighter *James* sometimes well out in front of the *Gabriel*. The *James* reached the waters off the coast of New England on August 8 and continued to Richmond's Island two days later, now a good three days ahead of the more heavily laden

Massachusetts Bay Colony's sea frontage usually provided easy shipping and transportation access. (Courtesy USHistoryImages.com)

*Gabriel.* By August 12, the *James* had already met "a fresh gale," according to a passenger, the Reverend Richard Mather, who kept a careful and thorough journal of the ocean crossing. Neither Mather nor Captain Taylor could know that they had met with the northernmost edges of the approaching storm, supplying enough wind and rain to keep the captain from making progress toward the nearest safe port in Massachusetts Bay. On the evening of Friday, August 14, he finally put in at the Isle of Shoals, on what would become the border waters shared by New Hampshire and Maine.

"Friday morning y' wind was strong at south-southwest, and so continued till toward evening, and then was somewhat milder," Mather noted. "But y' evening by moone-light about 10 of y' o'clock wee came to ancre at y' Iles of Shoales, which are 7 or 8 ilands & other great rockes; and there slept sweetly y' night till breake of day."

Early Saturday morning, the full force of the storm arrived. The wind shifted abruptly to the northeast, rain fell in great sheets, and high waves battered the shoreline and the ship as the hurricane's counterclockwise motion drove the sea forward. "Y' Lord sent forth a most terrible storme of raine and easterly wind, whereby wee were in as much danger as I thinke ever people were," Mather wrote.

The crew struggled to keep the ship in place as three anchors broke off, leaving just one to hold it against the storm. "We lost in y' morning three great ancres & cables; of wch cables, one having cost 50£ never had beene in any water before, two were broken by y' violence of y' waves, and y' third cut by y' seamen in extremity and distress, to save y' ship and their & our lives," the journal tells us.

As the winds and surf buffeted the vessel and the sailors severed their last connection with land, the captain finally determined that they had no choice but to set sail and hope for the best. "W'o' cables and ancres were all lost, wee [had] no outward meanes of deliverance but by loosing sayle, if so bee wee might get to y' sea from amongst y' ilands & rockes where wee ancred," Mather wrote.

Once at sea, "no canvas nor ropes would hold," Winthrop tells us in his secondhand account. The sails tore away and waved in tatters from the masts, wresting control of the vessel away from its captain and crew. The storm drove the ship "within a cable's length of the rocks at Pascataquack," along the southern Maine coastline, and for terrifying moments, it looked like the *James* would be bashed to bits against the rocks. "Y' of y' fore-sayle and sprissle-sayle there was scarce left so much as an handbreadth, y' was not rent in pieces, & blown away into y' sea," Mather said. "In y' extremith and appearance of death, as distresse & distraction would suffer us wee cryed unto y' Lord; and he was pleased to have compassion and pity upon us."

Indeed, just as the ship seemed doomed, the eye of the hurricane approached their position and the wind shifted in a fierce pivot, coming from the northwest and driving the *James* away from the rocks. Somehow, the crew gained enough control to ride the wind all the way back to the Isle of Shoals. Here it looked once again as though the ship would veer into the rocks, but the able crew moved swiftly to drop a last remaining piece of the mainsail, losing the wind thrust and sailing less violently into close proximity to the shoreline.

Mather, for one, believed that the passengers and crew had achieved God-given salvation from the terrible storm. "When newes was brought unto us into y' gunrooms y' y' danger was past, oh how o' harts did then relent & melt within us! And how wee burst out into teares of joy amongst o' selves, in love until o' gracious God, and admiration of his kindness in graunting to his poore servants such an extraordinary and miraculous deliverance. His holy name bee blessed forever."

By noon on Saturday the winds had died and the last remnants of the storm passed. The crew sailed the *James* southward along the coast, bringing her around Cape Ann and on to Boston Harbor by nightfall on Sunday.

The *Angel Gabriel*, however, did not enjoy the same good fortune. It encountered the brunt of the storm on Saturday, August 14, at Pemaquid, on the Maine coast northwest of Monhegan Island, and the details of her being "burst in pieces and cast away in y' storme" at Pemaquid Point, according to Mather's journal, have been lost to history. Many of the thirty passengers survived, but three or four did not; one seaman lost his life, the cattle perished, and the belongings the ship had carried across the ocean all sank to the bottom of the sea. The account makes no mention of the other three ships bound for Newfoundland, but we can guess that they fared better in the gale—or that they were far enough behind that they missed it entirely.

Another ship met an untimely end in the storm, this one a "bark," according to Winthrop's journal—a three-masted sailing vessel (usually known as a barque) owned by a Mr. Allerton, with twenty-three people aboard. Winthrop described the fate of the ship's passengers, twenty-one of whom did not survive: "One Mr. Avery, a minister in Wiltshire, a good man, with his wife and six small children, were drowned. . . . None were saved but one Mr. Thacher and his wife, who were cast on shore, and preserved by a powder horn and a bag with a flint, and a goat and a cheese, cast on shore after them, and a truss of bedding, and some other necessities." Thacher and his wife managed to survive with these meager provisions for three days on the shores of Cape Ann. "The man was cast on shore, when he had been (as he thought) a quarter of an hour beaten up and down by the waves, not being able to swim one stroke," Winthrop wrote, "and his wife sitting in the scuttle of the bark, the deck was broke off, and brought on shore. . . . One of the children was then cast dead on shore, and other rest never found."

The 1635 hurricane had the power to wipe out sections of Plymouth Colony. (Courtesy Library of Congress)

After three days, a search party in a small coastal boat (known as a shallop) came upon Mr. and Mrs. Thacher and rescued them. Only then did they discover that they were the sole survivors of the wreck of their barque, "so as there did appear a miraculous providence in their preservation," Winthrop finished with a flourish. He noted in addition that the "general court" awarded Thacher £26.13.4 for his trouble, a tidy sum that probably allowed him to replenish the goods he and his wife lost in the maelstrom.

The native people along the coast saw some losses in the storm as well, though they did not receive the careful documentation the European colonists warranted. Winthrop noted that the tide at Narragansett, at the southern shore of Rhode Island, rose fourteen feet higher than normal and wiped out a small neighborhood of "eight Indians flying from their wigwams." Chances are that others perished among the high tides and falling trees, but their stories did not appear in any of the journal entries that remain from this time in history.

## CHAPTER TWO

# "An Horrid Snow"— The Great Snow of 1717

Cotton Mather's historical legacy spans a remarkable number of fields, from religion to law to science, with his views on witchcraft securing him a permanent place in New England's history. A Puritan clergyman with a strong belief that witches were not only real, but sane, evil practitioners of black magic, he played a key role in putting together the bench for the Salem witch trials to ensure that the defendants received convictions and death sentences. Mather also worked to bring the first smallpox vaccination techniques to Boston, which seemed to stem the spread of the deadly disease throughout the city in 1721.

In between all these activities, Mather kept copious records of his and others' experiences in colonial Massachusetts, writing in his journal and sending correspondence to colleagues that would fill volumes when compiled by historians a century or more later. Thanks to the minister and his prolific pen, we have one detailed account of a series of blizzards in February and March 1717, written months after the fact but with plenty of residual drama.

On February 20, he began his account, "There came on a Snow, which being added unto what had covered the ground a few days before, made a thicker mantle for our Mother than what was usual: And ye storm with it was, for the following day, so violent as to make all communication between ye Neighbors every where [*sic*] to cease."

Unable to cross from one side of a street to the other in snow depths that measured in feet, people found themselves essentially trapped in their homes, floundering their way through drifts to tend to their livestock. "Ye poor Women, who happened in this critical time to fall into

Cotton Mather. (Courtesy USHistoryImages.com)

Travail, where putt unto Hardships," Mather waxed cryptically, perhaps referring to expectant mothers going into labor in the midst of the heavy snowfall.

One snowstorm in Massachusetts would not generally fall into the realm of unusual, but barely four days later, on Sunday, "Another Snow came on which almost buried ye Memory of ye former," Mather wrote, "with a Storm so famous that Heaven laid an Interdict on ye Religious Assemblies throughout ye Country, on this Lord's day, ye like whereunto had never been seen before. The Indians near an hundred years old, affirm that their Fathers never told them of any thing that equalled [*sic*] it."

Historians, including Harvard University history professor Jill Lepore and veteran newspaperman William Dow Cram, have unearthed letters and diaries written by farmers and other residents, detailing a total of four heavy snows over the course of just nine days. Frances

Manwaring Caulkins, a historian of the late 1890s, found in the diary of a man named Hempstead a particularly specific account: The storm began during daylight on February 20 and continued throughout the night, all the following day, and well into the next night, "The wind all the time blowing furiously, and the drifts in some places ten and twelve feet high." The weather broke on Friday, February 22, though the wind continued to blow the snow into drifts and temperatures remained very cold. Snow fell again on February 24, as Mather had noted, and churches remained shuttered as people waited out the bitter cold and wind in their own homes.

Three days of moderate weather and sunshine followed, but on February 29, the snow fell for hours once again, and it repeated this performance two days later on March 2—but with a rise in temperature that brought rain, beginning a long, messy period of melting and freezing.

Historian William Dow Cram discovered a journal from an unnamed source who was an eyewitness to the long snow siege. "Storm after storm swept down on the country and village until two weeks had elapsed," the diligent recorder wrote. "Finally when the sun did come out and the skies became clear, what a sight was before people! Snow lay at a depth of from ten to twenty feet." The man became particularly fascinated by the behavior of wild animals in the area. "The snow storm had its effects upon the animals and drove wolves, foxes, bears and wildcats to the settlements," he wrote. "These animals made raids upon the sheep pens and hog pens, and in some places so much were the deer harassed that the farmers cleared places and setup carts, fence rails and other barriers so that the deer could run in and be safe from the wild creatures."

The clearing sky and cessation of snowfall only revealed greater woes, the writer went on. "It was not an uncommon thing, just after the storm, for searching parties to go hunting for neighbors, lose their bearings and not able to locate the houses," so deep were the drifts. "Or perhaps a little smoke, curling upward through a hole in the snow, would show where the chimney was. . . . Most of the houses in fact were covered to the third story windows on the wind shaken side, and the barns were entered through the windows or traps to the hay lofts, the doors being so deeply buried that they could not be shoveled out."

Cotton Mather's grandfather, Richard, had survived the hurricane of 1635, and his father, Increase, had seen his share of major storms and other acts of nature in his lifetime as a New Englander, so we can be fairly certain that Cotton also knew that snow could pile up fairly high over the course of a northeastern winter. What made this one unique, the minister told his correspondent, was the effect it had on cattle—hundreds or even thousands of animals buried beneath weighty snowfall.

"Vast numbers of Cattel [sic] were destroyed in this Calamity," he said. "Whereof some there were, of ye Stranger sort, were found standing dead on their legs, as if they had been alive many weeks after, when ye Snow melted away." The rapidly falling snow created whiteout conditions that blinded herds of cattle, freezing their eyes and lashes so they could not see their way across a field. Unable to find their own way to safety, some of them walked right into the ocean and drowned, while others stood still as the snow piled up around them.

"One gentleman, on whose farms were now lost above 1100 sheep, which with other Cattel, were interred . . . in the Snow, writes me word that there were two Sheep very singularly circumstanced," he went on. "For no less than eight and twenty days after the Storm, the People pulling out the Ruins of above an 100 sheep out of a Snow Bank, which lay 16 foot high, drifted over them, there was two found alive, which had been there all the time, and kept themselves alive by eating the wool of their dead companions." The farmer returned these two resourceful sheep to the barn and pasture, where, Mather reported, they regained their own wooly coats and still lived as he wrote.

"Sheep were not ye only creates that lived unaccountably, for whole weeks without their usual sustenance, entirely buried in ye Snowdrifts," Mather continued. He told stories of hogs emerging from a snowbank after twenty-seven days, poultry discovered alive a week after the storm, and even turkeys dug out from snowbanks more than three weeks after they had been buried by the snowfall, "and at a distance from ye ground, and altogether destitute of anything to feed them."

We can imagine that entire neighborhoods and villages worked for days to dig through the towering snowdrifts and release people from their own homes, especially those who could not climb out a high

A blinding snowstorm disrupted life in colonial New England for days in 1717. (Courtesy USHistoryImages.com)

window and begin the process for themselves. "Every village organized searching parties to hunt for widows or elderly people who could not care well for themselves, and many cases were found where the people were starting to burn their furniture as they could not get to the wood shed for fuel," the unnamed diarist wrote, according to Cram. "Marketing was out of the question and many villages that depended upon the outside farmer bringing in supplies had to send out boys with sleds to haul in butter, eggs, milk and other provisions. It was great fun for the boys, coasting and fumbling about in the deep snow, but it was a serious business for the 'grown ups.'"

On Sunday, March 3, some parishioners dared to leave their homes and brave the high drifts and icy surfaces to attend church. A sermon given in New London, Connecticut, by Pastor Eliphalet Adams has survived all these years later, with the promising title, "A Discourse

Occasioned by the late Distressing Storm, Which Began Feb. 20, 1716 [Old Style],* 17," did not bring much comfort to the people who had experienced great losses of livestock and property. Pastor Adams centered his sermon on the Old Testament Book of Nahum, 1:3: "The Lord hath His Way in the Whirlwind, and in the Storm, and Clouds are the Dust of His Feet."

Adams suggested that the storm "shewed the Divine Displeasure yet more Visibly therein," calling out the probability that God meant to punish this congregation of New Englanders. He noted that the heavy snow had come late in the season, when "we were comforting ourselves that we had almost gotten through the Winter, which indeed had been very Moderate till then." The Lord meant to break the community's spirit by casting them "back into all the Solitudes and Difficulties of the Winter again," sending its residents the greatest amount of snowfall they had ever seen—enough to prevent "stirring from our Places about our Necessary Business or providing ourselves with those Conveniences of Life which yet it is very Uncomfortable to want."

The repeated blows of one storm after another also indicated God's wrath, "and we might well perceive the goings forth of him that is Everlasting in his sore Indignation against us by the mighty Dust of his feet." The fact that the snow actively prevented parishioners from attending church one Sunday also proved the Divine's displeasure, signifying that God did not want their worship until they "had Amended their Ways and Doings." Adams then acknowledged the "considerable Losses in their Substance and their Cattel. How have they Perished in Droves and been swept away in great Numbers by one Desolating Stroke!" This, too, came at the hand of their deity, however, as further admonishment for their sins. The pastor concluded his sermon with a thin ray of hope, asking God to restore all the residents had lost in the string of blizzards as a demonstration of His forgiveness after this repentance and cleansing of their souls.

"May the late Tempest that hath been upon us, tend to allay the Storms that rage in our Breasts and make us Meek, Peaceable, Gentle

---

*"Old Style" refers to the use of the Julian calendar before conversion to the Gregorian calendar. The British colonies' conversion to the New Style in 1752 moved colonists' calendar forward by one year.

towards all men and Easie [*sic*] to be Intreated, such as Christianity Describes and requires its Professors to be," he finished with a merciful flourish, no doubt leaving his congregation bewildered and perhaps furious at an unjust and wrathful God. With the understanding that the Creator could take away in an afternoon what had taken them a lifetime to build, they began the process of reassembling their own lives, secure in the notion that God most likely would be little help to them as they did so, and might one day sweep away all they had if they transgressed from a righteous path.

## CHAPTER THREE

# "A Most Tremendous Roar"— The Four-State Tornado Swarm of 1787

Northampton, August 22. . . . A large barn, belonging to the Reverend Mr. Russell . . . well filled with hay and grain, was entirely taken about six feet from the foundation and torn to pieces; some of the spars were carried as much as twenty rods from the spot where the barn stood.

—*Vermont Journal*, August 27, 1787

When people in New Britain, Connecticut, looked toward the south to determine the source of a sudden wind on August 15, 1787, they saw something no one in New England had seen there before.

"There had been . . . quite a strong breeze from the south, and about noon a cloud somewhat similar to those accompanying violent thunder showers, unusually black, ranged along the horizon from the north to the west, reaching about one-third up to the zenith, and its upper edge being indented and forming irregular columns, like pyramids," historian Sidney Perley wrote more than a century later. "It was different from the common thunder cloud, being one continuous sheet of vapor and not a collection of small clouds."

Some New Britain residents rushed to the tops of hills to get a better view of the strange mass coming toward them. "They saw a column of black cloud, about thirty rods [about 165 yards] in diameter, reaching from the earth to the cloud above," Perley said. "It was so dense that the eye could not penetrate it, and it appeared luminous, peals of thunder coming from it, which grew louder as it advanced. It whirled along with great force and rapidity, and was productive of an awful roar, that caused feelings of terror to arise in all hearts."

Perley called this a cyclone—another name for a hurricane—based on the fact that these funnel clouds appeared in several far-flung places at once, making it seem like one huge storm rather than several smaller ones. This dark, menacing column could only be a tornado, however, a rotating manifestation of a thunderstorm that funnels the storm down to the ground with violent force. New England does not normally see tornadoes on a seasonal basis, making this one particularly terrifying to those who spotted it and watched its forward momentum.

The first twister did "little damage until it shifted its course more to the northward; which direction brought it through the centre of the town of Thompson, where it tore up almost everything in its way," the *Vermont Journal* recapped on August 27, 1787. "It continued its course through the town of Gloucester with the same ferocity, taking up groves of wood, orchards, and buildings of every kind which came in its way."

A single tornado brought with it enough power and destruction to leave New Englanders breathless and afraid of what might happen next, but when reports of other twisters from the same day began to appear in newspapers throughout the region, people realized just how widespread and wild their impact was. One of the most vivid of these accounts came from Weathersfield, Connecticut, as reported by J. Lewis in the *Connecticut Courant* on August 20, 1787.

Wait Robbins had left his farm that morning with two of his sons to enroll one in Dartmouth College in New Hampshire. He left behind his wife, five children including a five-month-old baby, an older servant, and a hired hand. The family spotted the tornado coming toward them but regarded it more as a curiosity than a menace . . . until they saw it pick up a horse and throw it through the air.

Mrs. Robbins scooped up her baby and began to run, two of her young sons and the hired hand racing behind her. Suddenly, the hired hand met the tornado's wind head-on, and it lifted him off the ground, flung him high, and dropped him over a fence. He was not seriously injured, but the two boys were not so lucky. They were found "amidst the rubbish of the demolished buildings—the oldest, about 10 years of

Rudimentary agricultural tools of the late 1700s. (Courtesy USHistoryImages.com)

age lifeless—the other it is feared mortally wounded—Mrs. Robbins with her babe still in her arms is supposed to be hurled by the violence of the hurricane twenty yards back toward the house for there she was found dead, with her babe lying a few paces distant, wounded but not badly—The servant with the other two children fled a different course; they were all wounded but likely to recover."

Not only did the tornado take the lives of at least two family members, but it leveled the Robbins' house, barn, cider mill, hay pressing building, and their orchard, and it suctioned up three ox plows and carried them for some distance—two of which were never relocated. The remains of these structures were scattered across the countryside, including two silk dresses Mrs. Robbins owned, ripped from her wardrobe and carried by the wind for three miles, until they landed in Glastonbury . . . on her own brother's stoop. Mr. Robbins received the news of his family's misfortune from a messenger who tracked him down in Dartmouth that evening.

The Robbins family bore the brunt of the damages as the tornado passed directly through their land, but they were not the only ones in Weathersfield who suffered in the storm. A Mr. Rockwell lost a barn and the roof of his house. Trees throughout this section of town underwent significant rearrangement, some of them "twisted off and carried more than twenty rods [110 yards] without striking the ground," according to Perley. Horses and cattle were injured, some of them fatally. "It was exceedingly fortunate for the town that the path of the cyclone was taken where it would do the least injury," Perley noted. "If it had gone half a mile either to the right or left it would probably have been fatal to a large number of people, and a mile and a half farther in either direction would have swept the centre of the town on the north, or the centre of the parish on the south, and probably hundreds would have been killed or wounded."

When the weekly newspapers across southern New England began to circulate the following Wednesday, people in Weathersfield found that they had not been alone in their losses—and that the tornado that inflicted such damage to their village was far from an isolated incident.

"Last Wednesday afternoon a Tornado happened in several towns in the county of Middlesex," a report from Boston told readers of the *Philadelphia Gazette*. "It began at Cranes Swamp, in Westborough, and crossed the S.W. corner of Marlborough, where it unroofed the house of Elisha Maynard, and destroyed his barn; it then crossed the N.W. part of Southborough, where it unroofed one house, carried off Hezekiah Fay's cyder-mill, all the trees in his orchard except five or six, and Benjamin Parker's barn." The indiscriminate destruction continued: "It then went through the west part of Farmingham, where it took up from the foundation the house of the widow Shadduck, in which she and her sister were carried about eight rods [forty-four yards], and both very badly wounded, the house being dashed to pieces."

A report from Providence, Rhode Island, told of the northern section of town being torn to shreds as yet another tornado passed through it. The unnamed reporter for the *Pennsylvania Packet* called the twister "more extraordinary and terrible in its effects than anything of the kind ever known here." Townspeople first spotted it in Killingly, moving east by north, and "in its progress it tore up whole orchards by the roots; one large new barn, full of hay, was laid level with the ground; one old house and barn torn to pieces, the family escaped by taking to the cellar; one corn crib was taken up and carried about 4 rods [twenty-two yards]." More houses lost their roofs, a forest was "prostrated in almost every direction, and whole groves swept down." Witnesses saw long stretches of fence flattened, chimneys lopped off homes, and "vast numbers of stacks of hay were torn to pieces." This scattering of harvested crops would mean long-lasting hardships for farmers as they scrambled to replace the food stores for their cattle and livestock.

"Nothing in its way escaped its violence," said the report, but then it concluded, "We are happy to learn that no lives are lost, so far as we have yet heard."

A house in East Windsor owned by John Stoughton lost its roof, as well as a substantial amount of the family's furniture, which sailed off on the twisting wind. In Glastonbury, William Moseley lost his barn, while neighbor Theodore Gale saw his barn and house unroofed handily.

"At Gloucester, R.I., the [tornado] was more terrible in its effects than anything of the kind that had ever been known there," Perley said. "Several houses had their roofs taken off, and were otherwise much damaged. A large new barn, full of hay, was levelled with the ground, and an old house and another barn were torn to pieces. In the house were the family, who escaped injury by fleeing to the cellar." Chimneys, corncribs, and trees became flying projectiles, as did "rocks weighing several pounds" and other objects usually held in place by gravity.

One of the most terrifying stories came from Framingham, where a tornado lifted an entire house, "whirled [it] to some distance, and dashed [it] to pieces." Two women had remained inside the house as it rose from the ground and sailed, *Wizard of Oz*-style, through the air in the tornado's grip. They were "very dangerously injured," Perley said, and their household goods and furniture were scattered for miles. "A pewter plate was blown half a mile," he noted. The twister lifted a cart loaded with hay and pulled by two oxen, taking the entire team as a unit—including the young boy riding atop the cart—and sailed "six rods [thirty-three yards], the hay being scattered broadcast over the country."

Still more stories emerged in the weeks following the event. Reports came from Oakham, Massachusetts, where James Hasset and his family had been trapped inside their home while the tornado tossed its roof aside and scrambled the furnishings and people within it, then continued to his barn and "entirely destroyed" it, "not a timber being

In 1787, no one in New England had ever seen an approaching tornado. (Shutterstock)

left whole." People of Northborough, Massachusetts, may have seen the most extraordinary sight in the entire region: two columns of "black, fuliginous vapour instantly ascended from the point of coalescence, much resembling the quickened motion of fine smoke disgorged from the chimney of an air furnace." People watching this take place became quite speechless, the reporter said, as they waited to see what the outcome of this strange cloud behavior could possibly be. "Clouds of different appearances flew in almost every direction to that vortex, as a common centre, and were immediately wrapped in blackness," he wrote. "The whole hemisphere was great agitated, and appeared nothing to that war of Elements. Every beholder was interested, and felt anxious for the result, 'till the clouds from the east gave way, and then such a picture of devastation was drawn through several towns, so that part of Heaven had previously seemed to meditate."

The resulting column moved east through Northborough, Marlborough, Framingham, and Southborough with tremendous force, carving out its own path regardless of what obstacles lay before it, and leaving a trail of destruction "not more than 30 or 40 rods wide," or about 165 to 220 yards. Homes, barns, and occasionally people fell in its wake. Shingles whizzing through the air became embedded in tree trunks, affixed permanently by the driving wind. Spectators watched as entire trees spiraled through the air and found new resting places miles from their original roots.

That same afternoon, tornadoes formed and touched down in Dunbarton and Concord, towns in New Hampshire, destroying a newly constructed house in Dunbarton and blowing its owner across one room and into the next. A ferryman in Concord found his boat targeted by the column coming up the Merrimac River, rising from the water's surface and flying with the wind until it landed, miraculously, on the water again. A family of eight in Rochester, New Hampshire, held tight as the tornado lifted their entire house and carried it "a considerable distance," then dropped it, shattering it but relinquishing the people inside. Two of them sustained bruises, but the others walked away relatively unscathed. A neighbor's barn disappeared entirely on the wind, never to be located.

Not knowing what else to call this columnar phenomenon—indeed, the names had not been formalized in 1787—the media of the time used "tornado," "cyclone," and "hurricane" interchangeably, as this eyewitness to the Northborough tornado did in the *Vermont Journal*: "The inhabitants of this country (whatever may be said of others) have seldom been shocked with such a prospect as this Hurricane opened to view, and it is impossible to paint it in such a manner as to give the reader a just idea of the original. Suffice it to say, 'twas dreadfully entertaining to see parts of buildings, shingles, boards, timbers in different forms, household furniture, limbs of trees, and indeed whole trees sporting in air, and darting a thousand ways in clouds, which looked like the appointed servants of a HURRICANE!"

## CHAPTER FOUR

# "A Moving Vortex"— The Great September Gale of 1815

Lord! How the ponds and rivers boiled!
They seemed like bursting craters!
And oaks lay scattered on the ground
As if they were p'taters.
And all above was in a howl,
And all below a clatter,
The earth was like a frying-pan,
Or some such hissing matter.

—"The September Gale" by Oliver Wendell Holmes Sr., 1836

For more than 180 years, New England remained safe from the violent storms that form every summer in the southern Atlantic Ocean. The great storm of 1635 faded into distant memory, a legend passed down from one generation to the next, undoubtedly with fantastical embellishments by those who could only imagine its fury. Faced with much more immediate challenges including a series of wars, independence from England, and a new government to build, Americans of the early nineteenth century must have felt confident that such a storm would not pass their way again.

Weather prediction still had not become a viable science, so the people of the tiny state of Rhode Island and along the eastern coastline as far north as Rockport, Massachusetts, had no way to know that a gale the likes of which had not been seen in nearly two centuries had struck the Turks Islands, off the coast of the Bahamas, on September 20,

This contemporary illustration gives us an idea of how the hurricane looked to firsthand witnesses. (Courtesy Library of Congress)

1815. In just two days since its origin somewhere in the waters off the West Indies, the storm whipped up enough power to reach Category 4 on the modern Saffir-Simpson Hurricane Wind Scale, sustaining winds between 135 and 156 miles per hour.

"Catastrophic damage will occur," the National Hurricane Center tells us about such a gale today. "Well-built frame homes can sustain severe damage with loss of most of the roof structure and/or some exterior walls. Most trees will be snapped or uprooted and power poles downed. Fallen trees . . . will isolate residential areas." It concludes, "Most of the area will be uninhabitable for weeks or months."

With no warning that such a system approached the southern coast of Rhode Island, residents went about their business. They could not know that the gale would reach Long Island on September 23 at about 7:00 a.m., but once it traveled into Block Island Sound and headed for Old Saybrook, Connecticut, the pelting precipitation along its northern edge alerted coastal residents that this was no ordinary autumn rain.

The rain fell for a full twenty-four hours, according to a careful account written by John Farrar, a professor of mathematics and natural philosophy at Harvard University. Farrar dedicated ten years of his career to maintaining records of weather he observed from his position in Cambridge, Massachusetts. After the long rain, he noted, "Early in the morning of the 23d the wind shifted to the east, and began to blow in gusts accompanied with showers. It continued to change toward the south and to increase in violence while the rain abated."

With the shifting wind came a redoubling of the storm's force. "Between nine and ten o'clock A.M. it began to excite alarm," he wrote in a report published in a periodical called *American Philosophical Transactions*. "Chimneys and trees were blown over both to the west and north, but shingles and slates that were torn from the roofs of buildings, were carried to the greatest distance, in the direction of about three points west of north." The volatile conditions strengthened "between half past 10 and half past 11. The rain ceased about the time the wind shifted from southeast to south; a clear sky was visible in many places during the utmost violence of the tempest, and clouds were seen flying with great rapidity in the direction of the wind."

Wind ripped through Boston and the area surrounding it, uprooting garden plants, and tearing fruit out of orchards to deposit them on the streets of other towns. About twenty trees on the Common in the heart of Boston fell in the gale's path. "The overthrow of these trees is perhaps one of the strongest proof of the fury of the tempest," the Boston stringer for the *New York Evening Post* reported to that paper four days after the storm. He added, in an effort to calm the rumors that Boston had been hit far more severely, "Before we proceed in our narrative we must remark that the hour of alarm is not the most favorable for accuracy of description; and assure the friends of the town at a distance that our damage, notwithstanding the severity of the gale, has not been so great as they appear in the microscopic descriptions circulated."

The same newspaper gathered reports from towns up and down the Massachusetts coast, and noted that a number of churches had lost steeples, chimneys and barns had been destroyed, and entire orchards had come up from the ground and lay prostrate and spent. "All the fruit was shaken off but being mostly ripe, may be made into cider," the optimistic writer continued. Then the tone changed: "In all places to the leeward of salt water, the pastures have been ruined by the salt spray, and the whole of the standing trees and vegetables so blighted and changed as to exhibit the prospect of destruction by fire and smoke."

"It was computed at the time, that no less than 5,000 [trees] were blown down in the town of Dorchester alone," Farrar noted. The storm drove so much sea water ahead of it that the salt spray ruined crops growing in its path, leaving them with the same blighted appearance that leaves take on after a killing frost. From the ocean shore to towns as much as forty miles inland, windows wore a coating of salt, both from the actual inundation of salt water and from the ocean spray carried by the wind. Not only did this affect buildings and crops, but it also turned ponds, streams, and lakes brackish. "In some localities fresh water was long a rarity, and it has been said that some of the springs did not fully recover from the effects of this deposit of salt for years," wrote Sidney Perley, author of the 1891 volume *Historic Storms of New England*.

Hurricane scholar David M. Ludlam pieced together an account of the storm's progress based on a variety of written reports he discovered in the 1960s. He noted that the area from the mouth of the Connecticut River to Cape Cod felt the worst of the gale, "sweeping in from the ocean out of the southeast . . . a tidal bore which rushed up the ever-narrowing valleys and mounted higher and higher. The action of wind and water over Fisher's Island off New London swept all the trees from the eight-square-mile piece of land rising only a few feet above the sea." Buzzard's Bay, the narrow corridor of land between Cape Cod and the mainland, bore the brunt of the impact. "The peak of the winds coincided with high tide, and the waters swelled within 15 inches of covering the narrow isthmus and creating a natural canal where the Cape Cod Ship Canal later was to be dug," he said.

The very air seemed to change color and texture, Farrar noted. "It was considerably darkened by the excessive agitation, and filled with the leaves of trees and other light substances, which were raised to a great weight and whirled about in eddies, instead of being driven directly forward as in a common storm." Perley further described the strange air quality, "which at about the time that the wind changed to the southeast was very oppressive and almost suffocating. Respiration was laborious and difficult. This was particularly noticeable at Worcester, Mass., where a hot wind seemed to envelope the town and render the air non-elastic."

The spiraling wind, never observed in a New England town in recorded history, gave Farrar the first clues about the composition of such a storm, its shape, and how it might take form.

He noted that the storm "appears to have been a moving vortex and not the rushing forward of a great body of the atmosphere," he wrote in his 1819 report. "Toward the interior it raged with less violence, and in Vermont and the western parts of New Hampshire, I am told that it was not noticed as particularly remarkable. Yet still further west on the St. Lawrence, the wind was so high as to render it extremely dangerous to be out in boats on the river. And what is still more remarkable, this storm began to grow violent at this place about the same time that it commenced near the Atlantic, and subsided about the same time." Farrar did not quite reach the truth about a hurricane's spiral shape, but his observations served as hints through which future scientists would understand the nature of these massive storms.

As Farrar watched, the Charles River "raged and foamed," with spray "raised to the height of sixty or one hundred feet in the form of thin white clouds, which were drifted along in a kind of wave like snow in a violent snow storm." Most of us would see such conditions as a reason to head for shelter, but Farrar and his colleagues could not resist the opportunity to feel the force of such a gale in their faces, so they hightailed it outside and into the wind. Their effort to brave the storm in the name of science—well, philosophy, as science was called then—left them powerless against the driving wind, and "we were frequently driven back . . . and were obliged to screen ourselves behind fences and trees, or to advance obliquely." Standing still became impossible, even when they "inclined our bodies toward the wind, as if we were ascending a steep hill. It was with great difficulty that we could hear each other speak at the distance of two or three yards."

While Farrar and his fellow professors tested their bodies against the mighty wind, the people of Providence, Rhode Island, found themselves in utterly unexpected danger. After crossing Long Island at Center Moriches and moving into Block Island Sound, the storm turned sharply east and headed directly for Narragansett Bay, where it focused its power in a potent surge directly up the Providence River. "In sweeping over such an extent of water it accumulated a dreadful and most destructive tide upon this flourishing place," Farrar observed.

The rushing storm surge drove sailing vessels out of the docks and up into the streets, carrying them forward into the city. Prows of ships burst through shop walls and windows, while homes suddenly became submerged or washed away entirely, with their contents tossed out and transported on the waves. "The great calamity which befell this town, was rather owing to the extraordinary tide which rose twelve or fourteen feet above the usual mark of high water, than to the greater violence of the tempest in this place," Farrar wrote, but whether the surging tide or the high winds and rain caused the devastation had become a moot issue. By 11:30 a.m., the moment of high tide, the storm surge had pushed Narragansett Bay a full seven and a half feet higher than ever in recorded history to that date, driving ships in the wharves from their moorings and directly into the city "with terrible impetuosity, toward the great bridge that connected the two parts of town."

The bridge "was swept away without giving a moment's check to the vessels' progress, and they passed on to the head of the basin, not halting until they were high up the bank," Perley wrote. "All the vessels were driven ashore, or totally destroyed. There were wrecked in the cove four ships, nine brigs, seven schooners and fifteen sloops."

When the winds finally subsided and Providence residents ventured outside their homes, they found parts of these ships in their yards and gardens, and one sloop standing fully upright in the middle of Pleasant Street. An insurance office building took a particularly impressive hit, with the bowsprit of the ship *Ganges* piercing its third story.

Sailors remained aboard some of these ships and did their best to secure what they could on shipboard while they defended their own lives against the gale. One brig became lodged against the end of a wharf with nine men aboard, each clinging to the rigging and bracing themselves for the death they must certainly have believed was imminent. Somehow, sheer force of will drove them to risk leaving the craft, crawling off the ship and onto the scrap of wharf that remained, and from there to the shore as slabs of roofs and walls from the buildings along the riverside tumbled around them. For precious minutes they crept through the wild shower of debris until they cleared the riverfront and made their way down a city street, where, finally, some of them reached a house that still stood against the wind. Men and women inside on the home's second floor opened their windows and pulled the sailors within

The hurricane drove ships on Narragansett Bay into the streets of Providence, Rhode Island. (Illustration by Arnold Green, 1885)

their reach to relative safety inside. The remaining sailors finally found a space filled with high but less turbulent water between two houses and jumped in, swimming with all of their remaining strength for the nearest land above the water line.

Once the waters receded, the people of Providence faced the daunting task of locating and burying their dead as well as clearing the debris, rebuilding their homes and businesses, and restoring their lives as best they could after such monumental losses. "All considerations of property soon gave way to a more important concern," Perley said. "Everyone in the more exposed parts of the town became solicitous for his own personal safety and that of his family and friends." He continued, "No one knows how many human lives were lost in Providence, nor how many cattle were drowned." Those who survived were soon relieved to see a contingent of about three hundred U.S. military soldiers arrive to guard their remaining property against looting, knowing that theft of what little the storm had left behind would be a more supreme insult than the storm itself.

"The loss of property [in Providence alone] was estimated at several million dollars," Farrar noted, or what might be as much as $50 million in today's currency. One report suggests that Moses Brown, a Providence merchant, may have experienced losses to his business of as much as $1 million in 1815 dollars—a staggering sum at the time.

"All the space which but an hour or two before had been occupied by valuable wharves and stores filled with goods, and the river than had been crowded with vessels, were now one wide waste of water raging and furious," Perley said. "Along the higher portion of land were heaped together lumber, wrecks of buildings and vessels of every description, carriages, and bales of cotton, mingled with household furniture, coffee, soap, candles, grain, flour and other kinds of merchandise."

The destruction of Providence, however, represented only a fraction of the damage this storm had caused. Streets across the region became impassable as the storm piled up the debris of collapsed buildings, and strips of shingles had whirled in the wind along with wooden boards and chunks of other materials, crashing through windows and, in some cases, knocking down townspeople and crushing them to death. In Bristol, down the road from Providence on Narragansett Bay, the record-setting tide swept all the buildings off the wharves, and then took the wharves themselves. The surge destroyed the grist mill that provided grain to the people of Glenrock, and the Point Judith Light-house fell, the large slabs of rock that provided a footpath to the tower lifting with the tide and moving off into the sea. New Bedford, Massachusetts, lost all but two ships at its wharf, as well as all the ware-houses on the wharves. Island dwellers off the coasts of Rhode Island and Massachusetts found themselves more isolated than ever before, their homes and livelihood stripped from them in the sweep of rising water. In Stonington, Connecticut, the tide reached an unprecedented height of seventeen feet above normal, essentially erasing the town from its small peninsula just over the border with Rhode Island.

The news from Worcester, reported by an unidentified writer in the *New York Evening Post* on September 29, supplied more dramatic descriptions of storm damage, "Not only the trees which have been reared by the hand of man for fruit and shade, but uprooting the sturdy growth of forest-trees, planted by the hand of nature, some of which have withstood the storms of a century. Chimnies [*sic*] and some whole buildings were blown down, and others injured by the falling of trees. Many windows were broken by the seed balls of the buttonwood or syc-amore tree, which were driven through them by the wind. We have not learned the extent of this destructive impact, but have traced a column of more than sixty miles in width, with nearly the same devastation."

The report provided news of New London, Connecticut, as well: "Nine stores, large and small, and five slaughter houses utterly destroyed; four small dwelling houses nearly destroyed, and eleven houses considerably injured; two rope walks blown down . . . several barns blown down; thirteen stores and shops damaged; six wharves built on spikes entirely gone, seven built with solid piers essentially damaged. . . . The damage sustained by this city is variously estimated; we should suppose from the general enquiries we have made, it does not exceed sixty thousand dollars." The writer closed his report by thanking God that no one in New London died in the storm.

Perley tells the story of a woman named Mrs. Dyer, who managed to escape what could have been her last seconds on earth. "Having become much frightened, she left her house, and stood behind a large apple tree," he wrote. "[A] young man saw her there, and warned her of the danger of standing beneath the tree, which was much more liable to be blown over than the house. She left the tree and had gone but a few rods when it fell prostrate." The young man's thoughtfulness saved her life, and not a moment too soon.

When the wind and rain had finally dissipated, and the inland-driven waters receded to their accustomed levels, townspeople and officials began to take stock of the widespread damage. Roadways from one town to the next lay strewn with the remains of homes and fences, and massive trees had fallen across many of them, the removal of which would occupy able-bodied people with hand saws for the next several weeks. Reports in newspapers throughout Connecticut, Rhode Island, and Massachusetts detailed the losses of homes, shops, warehouses, churches, wharves, mills, barns, silos, and other structures, and listed the people whose lives were lost. In Vermont, a state with no coastline, the storm's winds did not reach beyond its borders, but torrential rain for at least twelve hours filled streams beyond their banks. Bridges and dams gave way against the water's force in Brattleborough and other towns, and a number of grist- and sawmills succumbed to the rushing currents and capsized.

As people had done centuries before, however, the coastal towns and cities of New England began the work of recovery. The loss of trees seemed insurmountable at first as farmers and lumbermen surveyed the denuded landscape, but soon they began to gather the downed logs and

The gale destroyed a gristmill in Glenrock, just down the road from this one in Kingston. (Courtesy Library of Congress)

turned them into building materials, making plenty of milled lumber available to people who had no choice but to rebuild their homes and businesses. "Probably New England never knew another season of such building activity as prevailed in 1817 and 1818, the logs having been sawed in the winter of 1815–1816, and the lumber seasoned during the following summer," wrote Perley. "This occurred in hundreds of towns and villages, and in one case, at least, a church was erected on this account. This was the old South church at Reading, Mass., the timber on the 'ministerial' lands being almost wholly blown down."

A few years later, almost no trace of the September gale of 1815 remained visible across the region. Forests had begun to recover with successional growth, new crops replaced the salt-scorched old ones, and new buildings stood tall along freshly constructed wharves. Self-appointed historians gathered the stories, however, and their records and observations became part of our modern understanding of hurricanes, their origins, and their ability to wreak indiscriminate destruction across entire states and regions, with no regard for human-drawn borders or the labor of thousands of people to create orderly centers of residency and commerce.

## CHAPTER FIVE

# "Unbridled Madness"— The Great October Gale of 1841

Sacred
To the memory of
Fifty-Seven Citizens of Truro,
who were lost in seven vessels, which foundered at sea in
the memorable gale of October 3, 1841.
Then shall the dust return to the earth as it was; and the spirit
shall return to God, who have it.
Man goeth to his long home, and the mourners go about the
streets.

—Monument in Truro, Cape Cod, Massachusetts

If we read the newspapers from October 3 to October 6, 1841, we might believe that the storm that passed along New England's Atlantic coast during those days did little more than blow some slate off roofs and flatten a few orchards. Some boats ran into trouble, as the terse report in the *Boston Post* noted on Wednesday, October 6: "The [schooner] Colma, D. H. Cole of Salem, from Philadelphia, with corn, for Salem, having lost her anchors was run ashore near [Hyannis Port] last night, and abandoned by her crew. The schooner remained a few hours and then drifted off, and has not been seen since."

Slowly, over the course of the next few days, reports grew more alarming as editors across the northeast began to understand what had taken place.

The storm first made itself known along North Carolina's Outer Banks and in Cape Henry, Virginia, never quite making landfall but disrupting shipping traffic for the whole of October 2. Then it turned northeastward, moving up the coast and gaining strength, taking the same route that merchant ships used for rapid passage up the Atlantic coast.

Days passed before the full details of the storm's fury became clear. The gale arrived off the coast of Rhode Island on the night of October 2, and by morning it whirled into the waters off Cape Cod, lashing the Outer Cape and catching all manner of merchant ships bound for towns along the coast, preventing them from reaching Provincetown and making safe port in Cape Cod Bay or farther north.

"Its terrible reputation has lived long in the memories of Cape Codders because so many seafaring youths of the small ports along Massachusetts Bay and Nantucket Sound went to watery graves on that wild night on the George's Bank," wrote David Ludlum in *Early American Hurricanes 1492–1870.*

Sidney Perley's history book gives us the most vivid description, beginning at midnight on the morning of October 3, when the wind "blew a gale" and brought rain to Massachusetts and snow to New Hampshire. "On Sunday morning the sun rose clear, but it immediately went into black clouds, and the sky looked wild," he wrote. "At eleven o'clock in the forenoon a heavy sea was running all along the coast, and vessels were being thrown upon the rocks and beaches. The wind continued to blow all day, and at eight o'clock in the evening was still a gale. In fact, it did not produce its strongest force until two o'clock Monday morning."

Nantucket stood alone in the hurricane's path. A tiny island off the coast of the Inner Cape, it had served as a hub for whaling ships since 1835, and its few thousand residents enjoyed a comfortable prosperity from this, as well as from the island's use as a transfer station for commercial shipping. With no ability to foresee the great storm headed for the island, ships set out from Nantucket on October 2 and 3 for their various destinations to the north, south, and east, and were well away from land before they felt the winds freshening and gathering power to the south.

"A gale from NE to ENE set in and blew with tremendous violence for 36 hours," the *Boston Post* reported in its Marine Journal column on

October 7, "during which a fishing [schooner] of Hyannis Port, Capt. Cathcart from George's Bank, had to cut away both masts—reports having seen a sloop off the Cape, bottom up."

More descriptions of losses off the coast of Nantucket piled up in the *Post.* "The ship *Rose,* which was on the eve of departure for the Pacific and of course in complete order, broke from her fastenings at Commercial wharf, and drove on the rocky foundation of an old wharf at the South Beach, where she bilged and has received other serious damage," the report said. "The ship *Planter* also broke away from the same wharf, and drove far up the beach, whence it will be difficult to remove her."

The *Post* listed many others: the *Leo Pendleton,* a New York ship carrying a large cargo of flour for Boston, became stranded on the northern end of Nantucket in Coatue, "where she lies much exposed" and "partially damaged." Another ship beached nearby, the fishing vessel *Rolando,* with "no cargo, and no person on board." A sloop lost its mast and became grounded at Brant Point, its crew making it to land and surviving the ordeal. "Most of the numerous coasting vessels at the wharves received more or less damage; some were partly stove, others rendered leaky by heavy thumping, and others suffered various injuries in spars, sails, or rigging."

Unable to escape the hurricane-strength winds and driving rain, and overwhelmed by towering waves, schooners and smaller ships met merciless destruction as they were swept against the rocky coastline and battered to pieces. A smack called *Platina,* a fishing boat out of Barnstable, Massachusetts, washed ashore at Nantucket's Eel Point a complete wreck, with the fishermen nowhere to be found. At least five schooners met their end near Tuckernuck Island off Nantucket's western end, the wreckage drifting in pieces to the beach. The remains of three more were discovered grounded on Muskegat, a flat, sandy island just west of Tuckernuck.

Still the reports came in, perhaps telegraphed to the newsroom from points all along the seaboard as citizens had the opportunity to inspect island shores. "Mr. S. Winslow reports the following wrecks—sch. Canary, Goodell, from Philadelphia for Boston, cargo coal, on Swile Island, masts gone and full of water; sloop Patmos, Keiley, of Dennis, on Tuckernuck, no person on board; a mackerel fisher on shore at do [*sic*], no person on board; and another off N. Pond, same island, crew on board—will probably get off."

As widespread and dramatic as the multiple shipwrecks on its shores were, however, they represented only the beginning of Nantucket's hurricane woes. A "gentleman who arrived from Nantucket," according to the *Boston Post*, provided a detailed account of the damage the island's settlements experienced in the gale, as printed in the Nantucket newspaper the *Inquirer*.

A newly completed ropewalk extending along the wharves had been ripped from its foundation "and torn to fragments, leaving only the tarhouse and part of the hemp-house standing," the editor wrote. "Several smaller buildings, in exposed situations on the beach, were washed away or shattered to pieces. A great number of chimneys, some of them from buildings nearly new, were thrown down by the force of the wind."

Homes lost their roof walks to the fierce gale, and trees, flagpoles, and fences became easy casualties. The storm surge drove the tide to an "almost unprecedented" height, two to three feet above the wharves and into the streets, "strewing in various directions quantities of lumber, cord-wood and other buoyant articles."

Nantucket had not seen this level of destruction from a storm in more than twenty-five years, the writer continued. "We shudder at the expectation of sad tidings from abroad," he said. "Our whole coast must have experienced this terrible storm, and at some points perhaps the visitation was even more calamitous than with us. We have cause for thankfulness that in such a season of imminent peril no loss of life has occurred. During the night of Sunday, especially, when every building trembled under the pressure of the furious elements, there were but few families free from alarm and consternation. On that night, literally, not many slept without rocking."

Lives were lost at sea, however, and not just off the coast of Nantucket. The *Post* continued to detail the carnage as various ports up and down the Massachusetts shore recovered enough to report their condition. Ships arriving from England took a severe beating as they attempted to navigate through the gale, including the bark *Arab*, arriving from Newcastle just in time to brave the storm and surviving with damage to its sails and bulwarks. One captain reported a sighting of the

This monument to the 1841 hurricane's fallen fishermen stands in the cemetery in Truro, Massachusetts. (Courtesy Library of Congress)

hull of the schooner *Andes*, out of Salisbury, England, "dismasted and abandoned, foresail hanging to the stump of the mast, anchor on the bow, did not appear to have any water in her." The same captain added that his ship passed "a great number of spars, and a large quantity of lumber adrift" as he headed for Cape Cod.

The first accounts spoke of lumber, masts, bowsprits, and sails, but by October 9, less than a week after the storm had finally blown out to sea, the news turned more gruesome as survivors began to discover those who had not: "Fishing sch. *Bridge*, of Dennis, came on shore yesterday near Race Point," at the outer tip of Cape Cod, "and all on board perished, having been drowned in the cabin." On the schooner *Spitfire*, the unnamed captain and "a lady" drowned, while the other passengers managed to survive. The crew of the *Alice*, out of Plymouth, was not so lucky as it "was also found this morning high and dry upon the beach, a short distance N of Highland light, with no person on board. From appearances she must have turned over when she struck the outer bars, as both masts are broken off, bowsprit gone, and the fish and other things floating about in the cabin. The crew of course we suppose to be drowned, but as yet none have washed ashore. The vessel has bilged."

A description of merchant carnage in Gloucester listed ten ships that took heavy damage, enough so that their crews abandoned them to drift out to sea, most vessels never to be found again. "The only loss of life that was known, was that of one of the crew of [schooner] *Tangent*, who fell overboard from masthead," the report concluded. "Several other vessels, apparently coasters, rode out the gale with safety."

The storm pounded ships to rubble as far north as Portland, Maine, and Portsmouth, New Hampshire, where the gale also brought several feet of heavy, wet snow. "The vessel named Maine, belonging to Bath, parted her cables and was driven out of the harbor on Monday morning," Perley tells us. "She was forced into Massachusetts Bay, where she struck on Cohasset rocks at nine o'clock in the forenoon, and went ashore on Scituate Beach, becoming a total wreck. There were on board seven passengers, four women and three men, and the crew which numbered four. . . . The captain, his daughter, five passengers, including all the women and one man, and one seaman perished."

Weeks later, the *Post* still listed shipwrecks from the storm in its daily Marine Journal, as pieces of ships painted with the crafts' names drifted ashore. The newspaper detailed the discovery of the schooner *Forest*, out of Gloucester, which had been lost "with all on board, eight in number. Upwards of 40 children have been left fatherless in this single instance," the writer underscored the tragedy. "Part of her stern frame with her name on it, came on shore a few days since at Coatue, the inner eastern shore of Nantucket." A few days later, the paper noted that it had received word via the Gloucester telegraph service that the *Forest* had been owned by Giles, Wonson & Co., and "was worth, with her outfits, $3000—no insurance." The column provided the names of the eight crewmen who died onboard, all "industrious, enterprising and steady men, all belonging to Gloucester, and nearly all of them having large families entirely dependent upon their daily earnings for support. Thirty-one children have been left fatherless by this calamity!"

The arrival of the US brig *Consort* at the Brooklyn Navy Yard on October 16 warranted a news item in the *Post* as well, as it had been delayed for three days in Nantucket by the gale. The *Consort* had been anchored at Nantucket Shoal on a surveying mission when the storm hit. "During the gale she lost spars, boats, a bow anchor—and threw her guns overboard," the *Baltimore Sun* added to the story. "When the gale broke up, she was off Barnegat. She had returned to Nantucket."

The *Post* added a positive word: "Officers and crew all well."

The residents of Cape Cod, however, would find remnants of scuttled ships along the Outer Cape's pristine sand beaches for some time. "The beach from Chatham to the highlands"—the sixty-mile stretch of beach that is now part of the Cape Cod National Seashore—"was literally strewn with parts of wrecks," said Perley. "Between forty and fifty vessels went ashore on the sands there, and fifty dead bodies were picked up."

The tiny village of Truro, just south of Provincetown on the northern end of Cape Cod, bore some of the worst losses. Its fishing fleet happened to be directly in the path of the storm, along the southwest of George's Banks, when the wind picked up on the night of October 2 and the crews realized that they faced a major gale. They raised sails and made a run for waters off the Cape's highlands, but the ocean itself had other ideas: The surge of storm current carried them southeast, pulling them into direct contact with the rocky shoals that extend for miles around Nantucket. Seven ships all foundered and sank, taking their captains and crews with them. "Those unfortunate mariners were nearly all young men under thirty years of age," Perley noted. "Fifty-seven from Truro were lost and buried in the great ocean cemetery."

Captain Joshua Knowles of the Truro fishing vessel *Garnet* had made his way down to George's Banks on the advice of a fishing captain out of Dennis, who met the *Garnet* on his return trip and told Knowles of the fine catch he'd made there. He ordered all sails up in the light northeasterly winds, but by 10:00 p.m. the wind had shifted, and the crew began taking in sails, furling one after another as the strong wind became a gale. Overnight the wind tore their sails into shreds, and Knowles determined by sounding that the boat had drifted far off course and into the area where the unseen shoals were most treacherous. As one throw of the sounding rope after another told them that they were in grave danger of breaking apart on the shoals, Knowles sent the crew below and he and his brother, Zach, stayed on deck. They devised

The 1841 hurricane took many ships and devastated New England's fishing industry. (Courtesy Internet Archive)

a plan to use the wind to swing the ship around as they approached land, but just as they were about to execute this difficult move, a massive wave blew up above them and swallowed the boat in its grasp. The wave broke over the craft and left her on her side, carrying Zach Knowles overboard and into the churning sea.

In a moment of stunning clarity of thought and action, Zach reached out and snagged a scrap of the main sheet in his hand and hauled himself hand-over-hand back on board. He and Joshua rapidly assessed the damage to the ship, finding the foremast busted off some fifteen feet above the deck, pieces of the deck splintered, and the galley, bulwarks, and other essential chunks completely missing. Both men secured themselves to the ship with ropes and began cutting away everything that held the boat in the water on its side—rigging, remaining sails, spars, and chains—using the emergency hatchet the captain always kept under his bunk. Their efforts paid off: they managed to right the ship and set it adrift just as the storm began to ebb and the sea showed signs of returning to its normal rhythm. By this time, it was Tuesday morning, October 5, and the welcome discovery of some potatoes still in the hold allowed the Knowles brothers and the ten-man crew, still in their quarters below, to consume their first meal in two days. The break in the weather brought them good fortune as they flagged down another vessel—the merchant ship *Roscius*—and became the glad recipients of a full rescue. Captain Knowles made the difficult, but ultimately necessary, decision to cut a hole in the *Garnet*'s hull and send the scuttled ship to the bottom of the ocean, a fitting but dismal end to a schooner he had sailed for several years.

Just slightly less dramatic was the survival of the *Water Witch*, with Captain Matthias Rich at the helm. Perley's research tells us that the *Water Witch* spent the night of October 2 at sea about ninety miles southeast of Provincetown, while the other fishing schooners in the Truro fleet were farther northwest. When the gale reached them at about 4:00 a.m., Rich and his crew hoisted all their sails to move as quickly as they could toward the cape, but they could not maintain a straight course with the wind and seas forcing them away from their mark.

"The sun rose, clear, but it immediately went behind black clouds, showing two sundogs [*sic*], the heavens having a wild appearance," Perley said, mentioning bright spots in the sky created by light refraction through the heavy clouds. Sun dogs serve as warnings to sailors that bad weather is approaching, though the crew of the *Water Witch*, already in the grip of the storm, needed no celestial beacons to tell them this.

Sometime after 7:00 a.m., the *Water Witch* passed the rest of the Truro fleet and saw that they, too, struggled to make headway in the violent weather. The storm continued to punish the vessel as it fought its way northward toward Race Point, until Rich finally made the call that "they must make a harbor or run ashore, as he saw no chance to fall to the leeward." Rich made a decision that he knew could turn out to be suicide: he and the crew would push through to the first harbor they could reach; if they could not make a harbor, he would run the ship aground on a stretch of open beach. Perhaps once they achieved a stationary position, wherever it was, people nearby or another ship would spot them and send able-bodied rescuers to their aid after the storm.

For another hour and a half, Rich and his men battled wind and rain until they were certain they had reached shallower water, a sign that they could be approaching land. Rich began to give the order for a last run to the shore, but before he could get the words out, the wind blew up a massive wave that rose high above the ship, breaking over the deck and drenching the men and their sails. "The jib and mainsail were hauled down, and they lay under double-reefed foresail," Perley said, meaning that the men rolled down the foresail to preserve it from damage against the whipping wind, making an effort to control the boat's speed and direction.

When the storm finally subsided at about 1:00 p.m., Rich had his first opportunity to get his bearings visually. He spotted land "well along to windward," and thought again of running the boat directly onto the shore—but as the men set the jib and mainsail to do so, the wind caught the sails and tore them to bits. "The main boom and gaff went over the lee rail, and they tried to cut them away," Perley said, but soon the men saw that this could leave them in an even more precarious position. Instead, working as one, they wrestled the boom and what remnants of the mainsail they could out of the water.

Just as it should, the boat righted itself, the remaining sails swelled with the wind, and the *Water Witch* began skirting the Cape highlands, clearing them "with no room to spare between them," and sailing briskly off to Race Point. They reached the north end of the Cape, rounded the point, and sailed on to Herring Cove—the first harbor past the point—reaching it at about 6:30 p.m. For the first time in twelve hours, Captain Rich left the helm.

"When morning dawned, theirs was the only vessel in the cove," Perley added, a crushing realization that no other ships in the Truro fishing fleet had made it home the previous day.

Many more ships took damage in the twenty-four to thirty-six hours the storm raged in the northern sea, and the consequence of this in loss of life has never been fully calculated. It appears, however, that hundreds of sailors, fishermen, officers, and passengers died in what became known as the Great October Gale of 1841, and while the memory of it does not resound as distinctly as the storms that did the bulk of their damage on land, communities up and down the coastline never forgot their heavy losses of husbands, fathers, and brothers. Dennis, Massachusetts, lost twenty-six seamen; Yarmouth lost ten, and Harwich lost the crews of eighteen fishing vessels.

No community felt the losses more keenly than Truro, however, where the population numbered fewer than two thousand. The loss of so many fishermen brought the number of widows in the town up to 105, with 19 new widows joining those who had lost their husbands over the preceding years in other incidents at sea.

"The loss in this storm of the fifty-seven young men of Truro was the most serious calamity that ever visited the town," Perley said. "There was scarcely a person but to whom some of them were related; thus making it in the most literal sense a public bereavement."

The obelisk that bears their names continues to stand today in the Truro Congregational Church cemetery. The tragedy had an even more significant long-term effect, however: for decades after the Great October Gale, young women of Truro refused to marry men who made their living at sea.

## CHAPTER SIX

# "Incalculable Loss"— The Great Nantucket Fire of 1846

The flames spread with such rapidity as to baffle every exertion to repress them; the expedient of blowing up houses was resorted to as the only means to arrest the conflagration, but it would seem with little success. More than twenty buildings were thus destroyed, and indeed many more would have been but that all the powder in the place was consumed.

—Warder Office, Nantucket
Tuesday, July 14, 1846, 7:45 a.m.

I t began in a stovepipe in the back of a store sometime around 11:00 p.m. Some accounts, including the one in the *Nantucket Warder* newspaper later that week, said it was W. H. Geary's hat store, while others blame E. & J. Kelly's jewelry store, though the exact location and the surrounding merchandise made little difference to the outcome. In a town constructed almost entirely of wood and loaded with flammable oil, the harvest of the booming whaling industry, fire had every possible advantage to be carried through the streets, even burning on the water's surface in the harbor.

The night of July 13, 1846, brought Nantucket's reign as the leader of the global whaling industry to an abrupt and disastrous end. By the time the townspeople smelled the smoke and spotted the flames, the fire had already begun to dominate the town, leaping from one building to the next and destroying one-third of the houses, shops, warehouses, and wharves before dawn. Selectmen fought the flames alongside every

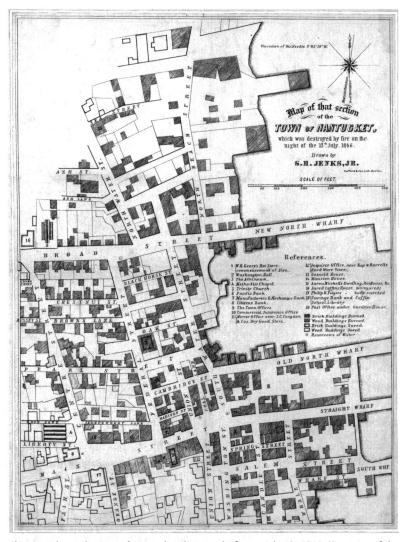

This map shows the area of Nantucket that caught fire on July 13, 1846. (Courtesy of the Norman B. Leventhal Map & Education Center at the Boston Public Library)

healthy resident and seaman in town, but once the flames reached the barrels of whale oil stored on the wharves, one explosion after another ripped through the town, spreading the fire far and wide. The contents of the burning barrels spilled into the harbor, spreading the fire even further, creating flaming slicks that could reach anchored ships. "It was exceedingly difficult to procure water, and the fire companies were quite unable to cope with the flames," the *Baltimore Sun* reported on July 17, based on eyewitness accounts passed down the seacoast.

The names of those who led the firefight have been largely lost to history, but sometime during the night these leaders determined that they needed to create a firebreak, an area already burned over that would stop the forward surge of the flames. To this end, they gathered all the gunpowder they could find and built charges in houses just ahead of the fire's predicted path. When they detonated these hastily made bombs, twenty houses blew up—but in all but one instance the effort turned out to be for naught. The fire simply burned across the charred remains of these homes, moving with aggressive haste to the next street, and the one after that.

When at last the fire found nothing more to burn, and those who fought it managed to bring it under control, the town stepped back and surveyed the damage. More than eight hundred people realized that they no longer had homes, and all their belongings were gone. The flames had leveled all the shops, storehouses, and markets, leaving nothing for the residents to eat or wear.

"The number of buildings consumed by the fire at Nantucket is said to be not less than 300, including 100 dwelling houses, and seven oil factories," the *Baltimore Daily Commercial* reported. "The loss cannot be less than a million of dollars; and but little insurance. The bulk of the insurance, out of Nantucket, is at New Bedford, where one office has $50,000, and at Providence, Hartford, and New Haven, and New York city."

The office of the *Nantucket Warder*, one of the island's newspapers, somehow managed to continue to publish as the fire raged on Tuesday morning, providing considerable detail to the *Fall River Monitor*, the *New York Evening Post*, and other papers on Wednesday:

> The town presents a scene of devastation that language cannot describe. The whole square of buildings bounded by Main, Centre, Broad and Federal streets is in ruins, and nearly all the buildings opposite those which formed the square. Trinity church is now in flames. All the buildings on N. Water Street, as far as

Aaron Mitchell's (inclusive), all the buildings on Main street from G. H. Riddell's to Straight wharf. On Union street as far as the building occupied by the Town's officer (inclusive). Washington Street as far as Capt. J. H. Pease's (inclusive). Dr. Ruggles's house on Orange st. was blown up, and arrested the flames at that point. . . . Many rumors are afloat of injury received by divers [*sic*] individuals, but they are so vague, and the whole town is in such confusion that it is utterly impossible to arrive at the truth. We are this moment told that no one has been seriously hurt. . . . We can give but a hasty account of this dreadful calamity.

When the *Warder* published its regular Wednesday edition on July 15, it provided "a full and correct record of the damage occasioned by the conflagration of Monday night," compiled by the editor of the Nantucket *Mirror*, which lost its offices in the blaze. It recapped the story of "the most destructive fire that ever occurred in this place," one that "diverged with a rapidity that appalled the stoutest hearts."

The account details the attempts to blow up houses to stop the fire's advance using thirty kegs of gunpowder—indeed, all the powder on the island, "but the fiery elements seemed to have gained the ascendancy, and for hours it appeared as though all human efforts to stop their destructive progress would prove futile. A scene of devastation meets the eye, that beggars description. Many persons have lost their all. We have no time for further comments."

The tally of lost buildings and services continued to unspool. The *Warder* contained a complete list of the people whose property now smoldered in piles of charred lumber. The *Monitor* reported that as many as four hundred buildings fell to the flames, including the post office, the printing offices of two newspapers, the Wing and Exchange reading rooms, banks and insurance offices, the fish market, and the offices of the county treasurer, register of deeds, and tax collector. Community meeting places, including the Episcopal church and the Athanaeum Library, a grand building that also housed a museum of "curiosities," had been destroyed, along with "many other valuable dwelling houses and stores."

In all this devastation, one bright spot emerged: no one had died in the fire. Several people suffered physical injury, but they were treated and recovered. "The crews of the U. States schooners Gallatin and Wave with their officers rendered effective aid at the fire," the Fall River paper said. The *Warder* also commended these men for saving what they could of the printing materials required by the Nantucket *Mirror*.

With a little more time for reportage, the *Warder* went out into the remains of the town to understand the extent of the fire's destruction and the effectiveness of the firefighting techniques townspeople had employed to try to stop it. In its Saturday, July 18 issue, it examined the methods for blowing up buildings to attempt to halt the fire's progress, determining that the structures chosen were "at points too near the property already burning. Had more distant spots been selected, there is reason to support that the progress of the flames might have been earlier stayed. But no one could foresee or even fancy the vast extent which the ravages of the terrible element were destined to embrace." Even several days later, the writer said, "one can scarcely realize the fact that so great a number of structures could possibly, by any agency whatever, in so brief a space of time, be thus utterly swept out of existence."

Exhausted, homeless, and bereft of resources to help themselves, the islanders had no choice but to reach out to the mainland for assistance. The town's selectmen sent an appeal to every newspaper in the near vicinity:

> Our community have been visited with an awful calamity. A large part of the business portion of our town has been laid waste by fire. A section embracing nearly all of our Provision, Groceries, and Dry Goods' stores, seven Oil Factories, a large number of Mechanics' Shops, and hundreds of other buildings, by which as many families are rendered homeless at very short notice. Many must be extremely destitute, and all of us very likely to be seriously incommoded by a scarcity of provisions which must shortly follow. Should you find it a reasonable duty to forward to a suffering community somewhat of your bounty, you may be assured that the distribution of such favors shall be promptly and cheerfully attended to.

Communities took swift action to help. The *Brooklyn Daily Eagle* reported a few days after the selectmen's plea that Francis B. Stryker, mayor of Brooklyn, had called a meeting "in order to devise some mode to raise some relief for the sufferers by the late disastrous fire at Nantucket." The officials decided that the mayor and secretary of the meeting would send a note to all the pastors of Brooklyn's churches, asking them to pass the plate the following Sunday for the benefit of Nantucket's residents. They appointed a committee of representatives from each ward to collect the funds and bring them to Stryker, who would act as treasurer of this emergency fund.

"If we may be allowed the suggestion," the *Daily Eagle's* editor urged, "we would impress on the minds of those who have this thing in charge—on the pastors and vestries of the churches, in particular, where the proposed collections are to be taken up—that the relief to be given should be immediate. We therefore think it best to have the collections, &c., taken up on the coming sabbath, 26th inst., rather than put off to the succeeding one. One hundred dollars now were better to the people of Nantucket than five hundred a fortnight hence." The editor also put in a word for individuals who had the means to make donations to the fund directly, rather than waiting for the Sunday collection.

Other cities clearly saw the need for swift action as well. The selectmen of New Bedford, the other major port for the whaling industry, held a meeting and organized a collection effort, and the New Bedford Railroad Corporation offered to ship goods and food to the island free of charge. At a meeting in Boston to plan the city's response to the tragedy, Captain David Thain, who lived on the island but was in Boston during the blaze, told the assembled officials of his arrival home the day after the fire:

> It is entirely beyond my power of description to picture to your minds the scene presented on entering our harbor, but you may form a faint idea of it, when I state that there was nothing left but a mass of smoking ruins, and chimneys standing without buildings, where, only two days before, I left not less than three hundred and fifty buildings. . . . My stay was so brief that it is impossible for me to give you any estimate of my own as to the amount of property destroyed; but a friend, on whose judgment and information I can place confidence, stated to me that it would

Only known view of Nantucket prior to the Great Fire of 1846, showing the north side of Main Street, with a partial view of the Pacific Bank and the Methodist chapel. After the fire, this block was moved back approximately thirty feet during the rebuilding to widen the square. (Nantucket Historical Association)

not fall short of $1,500,000. There is insurance on the property burnt to the amount of $320,000, which I have no doubt will be promptly paid.

The community of Pittsfield, Massachusetts, mobilized their donation collection force in a meeting at the Berkshire Hotel on Monday, July 20, and collected $571 in just three days, as well as seventy-five barrels and fifty half-barrels of flour. "The United Society at Pittsfield and Hancock, with the liberality for which they are distinguished when distress is to be relieved, presented the Committee on Tuesday morning with the generous sum of one hundred dollars," the *Pittsfield Sun* reported.

By July 31, the Boston *Liberator* reported that "the recuperative energies of the people are already at work, busy in repairing, by enterprise and industry, their fallen fortunes." Uninsured monetary losses originally estimated to crest $1 million (more than $30 million in 2021 dollars) had turned out to be about half as great as predicted, though a community as small and self-contained as Nantucket still staggered under the weight of such an expense.

It may seem that a tit-for-tat relationship would be entirely inappropriate between towns at a time of such loss, but such a discussion appears in the *Fall River Monitor* on August 8, 1846, less than a month after the Nantucket fire. One P. W. Leland, Esq., took it upon himself to correct "erroneous statements now being circulated by the public prints," about the level of generosity Fall River had shown to the beleaguered island—and how it measured up to Nantucket's aid to Fall River three years before.

Back on July 2, 1843, Fall River had faced its own conflagration, one that burned as much as twenty acres of buildings in the center of town. In the back of a warehouse owned by Abner L. Westgate, two young boys fired off a small cannon in an area piled with wood shavings, and within minutes flames engulfed the warehouse and several buildings close by as a strong wind carried sparks and embers along Main Street. "The whole space between Main, Franklin, Rock and Borden streets was one vast sheet of fire, entirely beyond the control of man," author Orin Fowler noted in his 1923 book *History of Fall River*. "Had not the foe proved the ally, the destruction would have continued until nearly the whole village was in ruins." The "ally" turned out to be the wind, which instantly changed direction just as the firefighters thought the town would be lost entirely. The gusts blew the flames backward and over the charred remains they had just consumed, leaving nothing more to burn. The flames soon dissipated.

The people of Nantucket stepped up for its neighbor in need and donated about $500 cash, as well as sending several boxes of "valuable clothing" and food supplies, Leland stated in his letter to the editor. This differed from a report that had appeared just a few days prior in the *Boston Post*, noting that Nantucket had donated $5,000 to Fall River's charity funds for fire recovery. The amount stated in the *Post* was most likely a typographical error, but Leland was eager to clarify it—and to crow over Fall River's greater generosity to the struggling Nantucket population.

Two weeks before Mr. Leland's letter, the citizens of Fall River met in the city's Market Hall and resolved that "as much was given us in the day of our calamity, much will be required at our hands, now in the hour of our prosperity." They formed two committees, one to raise money and the other to collect goods, and Market Hall became the central location for sorting and packing clothing and provisions for the afflicted islanders. "We will remember the liberality extended to the sufferers by the general fire in this place, in 1843," the newspaper summed up. "We would not forget the command—go ye and do likewise. Liberally we received—let us impart liberally."

It appears that in the time between the collection of goods and cash and the delivery of these items to Nantucket, some enterprising reporter got his figures wrong, making it appear that Fall River had not actually responded as generously as Nantucket had in 1843. Leland moved quickly to set the record straight.

"For the benefit of the Nantucket sufferers the citizens of Fall River contributed over $1200," he said. "The citizens of Fall River sent to Nantucket a few days since some fifty boxes of clothing, provisions and other useful articles." That being said, he added, "The people of Fall River have always felt that Nantucket did nobly, as indeed she did. On the occasion of the late fire at Nantucket, we performed our duty . . .

View of rows of whale oil barrels stored on a wharf. Four men are pouring oil through funnels into casks, most likely "topping off" the barrels. (Nantucket Historical Association)

both, under like circumstances, followed the dictates of humanity, and came nobly to the relief of the other."

The *Warder*, for its diligence in continuing to report on this story in the worst imaginable conditions, deserves the last word on this event. The editor provided his own lessons learned in a column on July 18 titled "Suggestions and Warnings," in which he decried the danger of "friction matches" and recommended widening the streets, building more structures out of brick instead of wood, and keeping wooden buildings at one or two stories to allow firefighters to throw water up onto their roofs to douse a blaze.

"Language is utterly weak and almost useless to depict the awfulness of the scene on Monday night, a night that will live in our history till the last tick of time," he concluded. "But the horror then, great and overwhelming as it was, is not to be named in comparison with what it would be, should a similar conflagration take place in a gale of wind, with the thermometer at or near zero. But, we have done. Our soul sickens at the thought. Fellow citizens, think of these things!"

The people of Nantucket endured, but its role in the whaling industry did not. Shifting sandbars off the coast and silt buildup in the harbor had already made the island's use as a port tricky at best. The fire flattened the services whaling boats needed, and while islanders worked hard and fast to get their commerce back on its feet, it soon became easier for whalers to head for New Bedford than to brave the hardships of Nantucket. By 1850, the island no longer served as a major industry hub. Decades would pass before Nantucket found its way forward as a tourist destination, restoring a level of prosperity and turning the lovely Massachusetts spot into a leisurely playground for vacationers and a summer home for wealthy individuals.

## CHAPTER SEVEN

# "Smashed to Atoms"— The Saxby Gale of 1869

It may seem obvious that the development of sensitive instruments to understand weather patterns became the technological marvel that made weather prediction possible. However, the turning point actually occurred with the invention of the telegraph, and the creation of a fully wired telegraph network in 1860. For the first time, a central laboratory at the Smithsonian Institution in Washington, DC, could work with data from far distant weather stations, gathered in something approaching real time. The farther away the origin of the message, however, the longer it took for operators to receive it, translate it into text, and then tap it out in Morse code, sending the information over the wire to the next operator many miles closer to the final destination. The process at each station could take hours, but represented an impressive improvement over transporting a written message in a stagecoach or on horseback over hundreds of miles.

These weather observers did indeed work with instruments that represented the leading technology of the time—barometers to check the air pressure, hygrometers to measure humidity, thermometers to indicate air temperature, and wind socks to provide the wind's direction and velocity. The Smithsonian took the leading role in distributing these devices and establishing the weather stations, creating the first systematic operation to attempt to predict the weather. The telegraphed messages then arrived at the Smithsonian from dozens of distant stations, allowing it to serve as the nation's central repository of weather information, where it employed a staff of cartographers and scientists to make weather maps and calculate the pace of storms moving across the continent. The weather forecasters then reported their predictions to government officials, newspaper editors, the military, and others who could make the best use of the information.

Today, we can check the hourly development of any weather system with a swipe of a finger on a smartphone, tune in to a local twenty-four-hour news station for a quick recap and forecast, or touch an app and see real-time radar images of a storm's current and future path. It's hard to comprehend that there was once a time in our history when the only warning a resident on the shores of the Atlantic Ocean might have had of an oncoming gale was the arrival of the storm itself. Indeed, before these advancements in technology moved weather forecasting into the realm of science, people had to rely on their own ability to judge what the weather might have in store for their homestead, town, or fleet.

Lieutenant Stephen Martin Saxby studied astronomical phenomena extensively in his role as a Canadian naval officer, seeking to keep the men at sea safe and give them ample warning of storms. In December 1868, he saw the confluence of the sun, moon, and earth coming together to create an unusually high tide in early October 1869—one that would have an effect far beyond the ships at sea. Such a tide, if combined with one of the frequent hurricanes that brought general havoc nearly every October, could devastate the coastline and affect people far inland as well.

Saxby wrote as much in a letter to the editor of the *London Evening Standard* in England, which was published on Christmas Day 1868, ostensibly to warn mariners who might be crossing the ocean the following October. His prediction meant little to those tending the harbors in the United States and Canada, however—the predicted tide was months away, and hurricanes happened every year; for the most part, people along the coast were prepared for such storms. No one felt the need to take extraordinary precautions just because another deluge might be on the way. Others believed that Saxby was making a forecast based not on astronomy, but astrology, a bit of hocus-pocus involving an alignment of planets to predict the future. They had little time for such nonsense.

As the new year came and went and October approached, Saxby realized that his first letter was long forgotten, and he wrote another one to the *Standard*, reemphasizing the enormity of what was about to take place. By now he believed a storm would develop that could gain intensity and become a raging hurricane, striking the eastern Canadian coastline just as the unusually high tide arrived. He wrote:

> I discovered some years since that neither the moon nor the sun ever crosses the Earth's equator without causing atmospheric disturbance, and especially in the winter months. The disturbance is greatly intensified when the new moon in perigee happens at such periods. . . . In October next all three corresponding causes will occur within a space of seven hours—i.e. perigee on the 5th at 7 a.m., lunar equinox at noon, and new moon at 2 p.m. So that even from these causes alone ought to expect in October increased disturbance; but this will furthermore be intensified by the circumstances of the sun's being nearer to us in October than it was on the 7th September by at least eight seconds of parallax, or about one quarter of his whole yearly change of distance. . . . Therefore, one is justified in expecting (to say the least) quite as great an atmospheric disturbance early in October as we have had since 6th inst.

Even with this dire warning, not many people paid too much heed until another authority, one Frederick Allison—a self-taught meteorologist with a weekly column in the *Halifax Evening Express* in Nova Scotia— reinforced the warning with his own letter to his editors. He predicted "a heavy gale will be encountered here on Tuesday next, the 5th Oct., beginning perhaps on Monday night. . . . Should Monday the 4th, be a warm day for the season, an additional guarantee of the coming storm will be given."

Allison went on to dispel the opinion that mapping the movements of the sun, moon, and earth amounted to nothing more than astrology. Allison added, "Apart from the theory of the moon's attraction, as applied to meteorology—which is disbelief by many—the experience of any careful observer teaches him to look for a storm at the next new moon; and the state of the atmosphere, and consequent weather lately, appears to be leading directly not only to this blow next week, but to a succession of gales during next month."

On the night of October 4, 1869, the forecasted hurricane arrived in the Bay of Fundy along the coast of Nova Scotia—and with it the predicted high tide. The result will forever be known as the Saxby Gale, immortalizing the man who saw it coming, a gesture of respect that served as a sort of apology for dismissing his insights for the better part of a year.

The gale produced a storm surge that overpowered every dam, dike, river, and stream for hundreds of miles, forcing seawater into waterways and inundating farmland and towns. With most farmers taken completely by surprise as the ocean water flooded their fields and pastures, livestock became trapped by deep water and drowned where they stood. Not only were ships in the harbors bashed against the shoreline and splintered into firewood, but railways positioned well inland toppled as the storm's high winds shoved a tidal wall across the landscape.

The tropical cyclone swept down the coast, inundating ports surrounding the Bay of Fundy in Nova Scotia and New Brunswick, as well as in Maine, reaching the thriving lumber and fishing port of Eastport on Moose Island at the southeasternmost point in the state. Eastport did a brisk business with cities and ports in the British provinces to the north, often hosting the crews of as many as two hundred to three hundred fishing boats and providing the vessels and crews with the provisions they needed to spend days at a time out at sea. It maintained a connection to the mainland over a 1,200-foot-long covered bridge, which led into the town of Perry, and residents and visitors often took a ferry from Eastport to Lubec or other northeastern towns.

Eastport had seen its share of storms, and its harbor had become the scene of shipwrecks on its prominent rocks in seasons past, but none had walloped the port town as hard as the one that arrived on October 4, 1869.

"The hurricane at Eastport was terrific, vessels, wharves, stores and fish houses were smashed to atoms," the *Evening Star* in Washington, DC, reported on October 11, a week after the storm. "Twenty-seven vessels got ashore in Romney's bay. The schooner *Rio* was lost in Romney's bay, with all on board. A bark at New River was lost with all on board, seventeen in number."

The *Philadelphia Inquirer* reported that the steamer *New York* lost both her anchors and rudder as the gale dumped the ship on shore at Eastport. "Many merchants here have lost all their property," it added. "J&S Griffin lost all their vessels, fish and storehouses. J. S. Pearce lost his store and all his stock. Most of our fishing vessels are in pieces." It went on to list nineteen ships that had been pushed ashore in the storm, noting, "All the smokehouses are down: immense quantities of herring and oil are lost. The loss cannot be less than $500,000. A large part of the town is a perfect wreck."

Somehow, the steamer *New York*, with two hundred passengers onboard, managed to run aground on a sandbank in Eastport's harbor instead of breaking up on the rocks. The captain and crew determined that there was nothing they could do during the fiercest part of the gale, and stepping out on deck at all would most certainly result in their being swept away by the wind and waves, so they battened the hatches and waited below for the worst to be over. In the meantime, a particularly towering wave crashed and broke across the hurricane deck, where several passengers' staterooms stood, loosening the deck and almost severing it from the ship. As the storm subsided, the captain and crew did their best to move the *New York* off the bank, but this only sent it into the still-roiling harbor and very nearly smashed it to bits on the rocks. Just at the point of impact, however, a wave rose and slapped the ship away, leaving her floating on the sea—much the worse for the experience, but with all its passengers accounted for.

A reporter from another newspaper shared a conversation he had had on the evening of October 11 with "a gentleman who arrived yesterday from Eastport," the paper said. "He says that the fury of the elements beggars all description. For three days previous to the hurricane, a strong west wind had raged without intermission. On Monday morning, the 5th inst., at about 9 A.M., what promised to be an ordinary autumn storm changed to a gale, and by 3 P.M. the gale was so fierce that it was impossible to walk the streets." The wind wailed in every crack, tearing away everything that was the least bit loose and hurling pieces of buildings and ships through the town. It built to a climax that began at 6:30 p.m. and continued for two hours, unleashing the worst of its destructive power on Eastport. "The flood-gates of Heaven were let loose, and, to crown all, the restless tide of the Atlantic came billowing up over the wharves until it seemed that the ocean itself was about to undertake the work of annihilation."

Now the wind wrenched oak trees out of the ground, reduced them to twigs, and scattered them in every direction. Some houses withstood the gale, while others came loose and sailed off on volatile gusts. The *Inquirer* reported that 150 chimneys snapped in half. "Nearly all the roofs were crumpled like rolls of parchment," the reporter said.

The lumbering operation at the Denniston Steam Mill Company lay entirely destroyed, including significant improvements that had just been completed. The river's flooding covered farmers' fields with ocean sand several feet deep in some places, taking out buildings and homes as it swamped the lowlands. "The farmers living on the river are impoverished and homeless," the *Inquirer* completed its report.

The many fishing boats in the vicinity when the storm began had all but vanished, the gentleman from Eastport told the newspaperman. "Sloops and schooners exist only in fragments, which are tossed to and fro on the spray," the paper reported. "Vessels of heavier tonnage dragged their anchors, and smashed the wharves, which they carried away. The seamen, to save their lives, leaped from the unlucky crafts to the piers, where they fell on their faces and held on with their hands. They could not stand against the hurricane."

When the tempest finally calmed in the wee hours and the darkness lifted at dawn, the rising sun lit a massively changed panorama. Homes, barns, factories, public buildings, and the wharves lay in ruins. Shipwrecks lined the harbor, their dislocated masts and spars protruding from the seawater lapping at the shore. "Our informant has a list of 137 vessels that he knows to have been lost," the *Inquirer* said.

The *Evening Star* listed Lubec, Pembroke, and Perry as additional coastal towns that took heavy losses of property and noted news of a "great freshet" in Maine's Swift River. "The stream is a tributary of the Androscoggin, and the rise was thirty-six feet in twelve hours in the neighborhood of Oxford county," the story continued. "The destruction of property was very great, and the inhabitants barely escaped with life, and fled to the mountains."

Higher ground was no guarantee of survival, however. Of the thirty-seven deaths recorded in the storm, one of them happened as far away from the shore as Mount Washington in New Hampshire's White Mountains. There at Glen House, J. M. Thompson, proprietor of the hotel at the time, happened to be out in his mill when the storm surge barreled down the Androscoggin River. The mill and the paddlewheel that powered it were positioned directly over the river.

"The rise in the Androscoggin River is unprecedented," declared a report on the massive flood gathered from telegraph wire reports by the *Daily Kansas Tribune* in Lawrence, Kansas. "Several millions of logs have gone over the falls."

Logs from an upriver lumber operation rushing down a swollen river sounds like the stuff of nightmares, but this is exactly what swept the mill off its foundation and down the river, taking poor Mr. Thompson with it. He drowned in the river, imprisoned by the collapsing building and the wall of debris driven by the current.

Just a few days before the Saxby Gale arrived in the Bay of Fundy, the *New Jersey Standard* proposed a system through which storm spotters could send telegraph messages to the next towns up the coast, warning them of the oncoming weather. Having this communication from people who could see the storm and gauge its force would save lives, the unnamed writer said, by providing residents, businesses, and ships the opportunity to prepare for the gale before it arrived.

The plan is as follows:

When a storm has formed, and commences to travel in any certain direction, the first telegraph station or stations, over which it passes, are to send the news to all the telegraph stations at cities, county seats and principal towns, scores or hundreds of miles in advance, according to the kind of storm, or probably distance that it may travel, always keeping a suitable distance in advance.

At each city, county seat and principal town, a cannon is to be kept ready by the officials at the court-house, or by a fire company, and as soon as the news is received of a coming storm it is to be fired three times, and intervals of one minute if a tornado, terrific gale, or any destructive storm is approaching; at intervals of three minutes if an ordinary rain or snowstorm is approaching rapidly; and at intervals of six minutes if an ordinary rain is approaching slowly.

The writer went on to suggest that once the urgent cannon fire had been heard in a city or town, the churches should ring their bells, steam whistles should be blown at factories and other establishments that had them, and fire companies should sound whatever signaling devices they had as well.

This may have been the first cogent recommendation for an advance warning system, one that could broadcast far enough and loudly enough to alert entire towns to the approach of a force that could change their lives in terrible ways. The arrival of a storm just three days later underscored the need for an early warning system—and while we can't be sure that anyone took this reporter's plan to heart, the telegraph had already become the first major breakthrough in weather reporting and forecasting. Its broadened use for alerting others to approaching storms could not have been far behind.

## CHAPTER EIGHT

# "Deep, Wet and Drifting"— The Great Blizzard of 1888

> With railroading blocked and telegraph wires down, [Bostonians] could not but ponder on the omnipotence of nature's laws. In their meditations, they could not but have been impressed with much concerning the march of progress in these later years. . . . Never before, perhaps, did they fully appreciate the luxuries afforded by steam and electricity in the modern days in which they were so fortunate as to have been born.
>
> —*Boston Globe*, March 15, 1888

"It Came From Michigan," the *Boston Globe* pronounced on March 12, 1888, picking up a report out of Negaunee, Michigan, from earlier in the day. For two days the Boston newsroom had seen telegraphed reports of a storm that dumped umpteen feet of snow on Michigan's Upper Peninsula and on cities as far south as Chicago, burying trains and stopping commercial traffic literally in its tracks. This news did not bode well for Massachusetts and its neighboring states, all of which had already experienced one of the snowiest winters on record.

"The first week in March has been conspicuous for a spell of weather that for low temperature would compare most favorably with a similar week of any normal January," the *Globe* observed on March 9. An early March storm brought considerable snowfall as it stalled over the northeastern United States, "halted by the high [pressure] area then prevailing over the north Atlantic."

Meteorological science had advanced significantly by 1888, giving the press the ability to explain weather systems in terms of high and low pressure. The *Globe* offered a lengthy analysis of the storm just passed and the one forming in the west, and then concluded, "For tomorrow for New England, generally fair weather, possibly light snows, winds shifting from northerly to southwesterly, warmer weather and later rain. Another fall of temperature may be expected by Sunday."

That's not quite how Sunday went.

Shortly before sundown on March 11, rain began to fall along New England's southern shores. As its final deadline for the morning edition approached late Sunday evening, the *Morning Journal-Courier* in New Haven, Connecticut, received a troubling telegram from New York City, saying that no weather report had been transmitted from Washington, and "all connection from Washington was shut off."

Inclement weather some three hundred miles southwest of Connecticut did not immediately cause concern in New Haven, though the newspaper office did know that a severe snowstorm had shut down much of the Midwest around Lake Superior the day before. The storm had arrived in upstate New York by Sunday morning, dumping twenty-one inches of snow on Saratoga, New York, by noon, and a foot of snow overnight in Newburgh in New York's Hudson River valley. It then headed directly for New York City.

By midnight Sunday, the temperature dropped into the twenties and the wind picked up significantly, bringing with it what the limited weather vocabulary of the time quickly deemed a "cyclone." On the wind came the snow, falling with "unabated fury," the *Boston Globe* described it in the paper's 5:00 p.m. Extra edition on Monday, March 12. "Snow is falling heavily and there is now four feet of snow upon the ground," it informed readers in Boston who, if they ventured out, were already up to their chests in the stuff. "All business upon the streets has been suspended, teams and drivers being driven to places of shelter."

At about 3:00 a.m. on Monday morning, the storm's full force reached the Connecticut shore and "continued to increase in fury as the day began to dawn," the *Morning Journal-Courier* reported on Tuesday, March 13. With little familiarity with storms of this magnitude, many New Haven residents attempted to leave the house in the morning and make their way to work. "Those business and professional men accustomed to being at their offices at eight o'clock or soon after did not put in an appearance until late, very late, and then began to query as to how much longer the battling elements would battle," the newspaper said. These working people made numerous calls and sent messages to the local signal and weather officer, a man named Sherman, begging for information about where the blizzard had come from and how much longer it might rage in their city. "Mr. Sherman was unable to answer most of the questions propounded, as communication with Washington was entirely cut off," the paper explained. "He gave all the reply that the storm would undoubtedly continue all day and be the worst New Haven had ever experienced."

Despite the lack of connection to the national weather bureau, however, Sherman did collect data firsthand throughout the night on Sunday and well into Monday. He determined that more than a foot of snow had fallen in New Haven between 4:00 a.m. and 7:00 a.m. Monday morning, and by 3:00 p.m., the accumulation passed two feet. "At 6 p.m., when the last measurement was taken, it was over three feet on the level," the newspaper reported.

By this time the storm had spread to the north and east, piling several feet of snow on other communities in Massachusetts, as well as in Rhode Island. The snow's weight collapsed telephone and telegraph lines suspended along city streets and throughout the surrounding area, cutting off Boston from the rest of civilized society. The *Globe* tracked its ability to communicate with other cities for as long as it could, notifying its readers that New York City lost its wire connections around midnight the evening before. "The few wires that are working to the East are liable to give out at any moment," the paper noted. "The signal service is helpless, having no information from any source outside the city, and only knows that as the barometer is still falling, the storm is still west or northwest of them. The last communication kept up between New York and the East was the Long Distance Telephone service," but even this finally "came to grief by a gale in New York city, somewhere between the Cortlandt-street office and King's bridge, blowing down and cutting off that last means of communication."

For the first time in history, residents of America's northeastern states experienced what it was like to be offline. Cut off from telephone

Snow in Hartford piled up ten feet and higher after three days of continuous snow. (Connecticut Historical Society)

and telegraph, people could no longer talk to one another casually across great distances, a luxury that had just recently become a staple of daily life. A silence descended over New York and New England, with only the wind's ferocity breaking the stillness. "The Western Union people have never known anything like the present blocking of their lines," the *Hartford Courant* reported on March 13. "The wires in all directions are either down or badly mixed. One wire works intermittently to Portland and another to Newport. With most points communication is entirely cut off."

Trains stopped attempting to travel along buried routes after a collision of two elevated trains in New York early on the morning of March 12 that killed the engineer of one and left the other locomotive "literally smashed to pieces," according to the *Globe*. Reports came in from New Haven that trains usually bringing the mail and newspapers out of New York were stranded at Black Rock, just before Bridgeport, "with not very favorable prospects of moving, as the snow packs hard and is drifting badly." On a rail line in Meriden, Connecticut, a train became completely stuck in snow that drifted across the track at the South Colony street crossing, "and though five powerful engines are striving to move it, at this hour (2 p.m.) there is no prospect of its getting in today."

Other trains did not even make it that far, getting wedged in deep snow before they reached Meriden.

Telegraph poles fell across the railroad tracks in Marion, and trains from Naugatuck and Northampton became trapped by deep snow. By 11:00 a.m., New Haven reported fifteen inches of "deep, wet and drifting" snow piling up in railroad yards, where drifts forced railroad crews out of the cars to shovel the stuff off the tracks—a losing proposition as the snow continued to fall. Wind swirled stinging flakes into their faces and carried the snow back onto the tracks as quickly as they could remove it.

"The railroad business is at a complete standstill," New Haven's report continued. It was blocked in part by a train that had attempted to get out of the yard and jumped the track, forming a barrier on both the outgoing and incoming lanes. "Several trains from the east have been standing in the cut for hours waiting to get into the depot."

On city streets coaches pulled by horse teams couldn't navigate in the deep snow. "On the horse-car roads, cars pulled by six and eight horses have become stuck and abandoned by the passengers," New Haven's reporter said.

Meanwhile, the volatile front kicked up the surf along Connecticut's shoreline, particularly at Crescent Beach, between Niantic and Attawan beaches. At the Vue d l'Eau Hotel, seawater covered the roads from Winthrop Junction to Beachmont and gouged away deep gullies in the road, and waves rose as much as twenty-five feet at the Deer Island breakwater. "At the hotel heavy seas strike the staunch bulkhead with a noise like the roar of a cannon," the report said. "The wind and sleet drive directly inshore, and give additional momentum to the waves and tide, which are dangerously strong and high in themselves. . . . The people living near the shore are in the greatest excitement as they fear the water will rise higher and flood them out of their homes."

Bad news from the Rhode Island shore at Point Judith also reached the *Globe* newsroom: the *McNeal, Jr.*, a schooner from Boston, and two other unnamed ships were dashed to pieces and "strewn across the beach. Shore property at Narragansett Pier has suffered, and the aggregate damage will amount to considerable," the *Globe* said. Four inches of sleet had built up on the telephone and telegraph wires along the

Connecticut shore, "and now that the wind is blowing the situation looks bad for telegraphic service west."

In Providence, Rhode Island, the snow came through and passed over the city by midday Monday, but a new storm followed with temperatures just warm enough to replace the snow and sleet with torrential rain. Businesses came to a standstill as communication from surrounding cities went completely silent. "The storm was terrific on Narragansett Bay, and at Newport it was the worst in years," the report said. "Block Island is storm-bound, and it will be several days before the regular steamer can reach there. The breakers there are rolling over the bluffs, and at the Springs and Sandy Point the seas sweep clear across."

The *Globe* looked to the weather bureau for a prediction of when the storm might abate. It reported that it could be midnight on March 12 before it began to subside.

Midnight came and went, but the storm didn't.

On Tuesday morning, March 13, the *Morning Journal-Courier* in New Haven reported that "the worst snow storm ever experienced in this vicinity" still blew as the paper went to press. "In the memory of the oldest citizen the like had never before been experienced," the news said. "Night came on, but its fury had not spent itself. As darkness shrouded all it rage[d] with increased ferocity."

Horsecars ceased to run in New Haven by noon on Monday, and only one or two of the trains in transit on Monday morning had managed to work their way through to their destinations. Overall, however, the city most central to the Connecticut shoreline lay locked in "snow, snow everywhere," as the newspaper's writer lamented, with drifts piled up to fifteen feet high. No one could get into or out of the city, as every road had become "entirely impassable. The prospects are that they will remain so for two days or longer if the storm does not abate this morning."

Somehow, despite the lack of electrical communication, the New Haven newsroom continued to collect reports from up and down the state's southern seaboard about trains reaching—or not reaching—their destinations. A train leaving New Haven at 3:50 a.m. Monday actually managed to reach Grand Central Terminal in New York just an hour behind schedule, but it was the last train to do so that night. One train left New London at 9:25 a.m. Monday morning, but it made it only as far as Fair Haven before it attempted to penetrate a "huge drift" on the track and stalled, effectively ending any train traffic on that track until the storm cleared. Before long, another train heading east made it to Fair Haven as well, but its engineer and conductor spotted the waylaid train stuck in the massive drift and knew that they would go no farther that day. "The train men gathered at the station and swapped experiences," said the *Morning Journal-Courier*. "The passengers on the two Fair Haven trains were cared for by the people residing in the vicinity."

An express train scheduled to stop in Old Saybrook at 11:15 a.m. actually reached this station just two hours late, but it soon became buried in snow and moved no farther. Conductor De Wolf quickly took charge of the passengers and shepherded them into the train depot, where they obtained a meal in the station restaurant and received offers from residents to provide them with lodging until the trains began running again.

Story after story of Connecticut residents lending a hand to stranded passengers reached the ears of the unnamed reporter waiting for word throughout the night with officers at the Union depot. When a freight train on the Northampton line jumped the track while attempting to ram its way through drifted snow, residents of Cheshire mobilized to collect the engineer McConville, the conductor Hart, and the train's crew and show them some warmth and hospitality. Citizens of Plainville did the same for a train stranded there on its way to New Haven, with its engineer Brown and conductor F. R. Smith making certain that the passengers had what they needed. "Everything possible was done for the passengers aboard," the paper reported. "Eatables were secured from houses in the vicinity."

Throughout that snowbound Monday and overnight into Tuesday, railroad superintendents O. M. Shepard and Wallace remained at the posts at Union depot, along with other officers and train dispatchers Beers, Penney, Giles, and Smith—and, apparently, a reporter from the *Morning Journal-Courier*, who did a thorough job documenting the whereabouts of each stranded train. "One after another of the stations along the line were cut off by the breaking of the wires, and at 7 p.m., they could reach nowhere," the unnamed reporter said. Despite the communication breakdown, Shepard received "intelligence from New

York" that all the trains out of the city had stalled at Harlem early Monday morning, and no others had attempted to follow them. "The storm was even more severe in New York, and snowdrifts ten feet high block the tunnel entrance, and it is entirely impracticable to move about the yards," the reporter wrote. The source in New York "was of the opinion that travel could not be resumed before tonight or tomorrow morning. He had never before experienced a similar trouble in his twenty-five years of service."

Conditions further north were no better, with trains stalled in Hartford, Meriden, and East Berlin. The one saving grace, Superintendent Shepard told the reporter, was the spring temperatures that hovered in the low thirties throughout the storm. While this relative warmth made for heavy, wet snow that weighed down wires and made railroad tracks impassable, the people stranded in trains or working to dig out locomotives could be kept warm enough to avoid real hardship. "As near as could be ascertained all passengers on the stalled trains suffered comparatively little from either exposure or hunger," the paper reported. "The trains were principally stalled where refreshments could be secured by the train hands for those in the snowed-in cars. There were light-hearted and jovial spirits aboard most of the trains, which made the position of the passengers bearable, and all rather relished the novelty of the thing."

One reporter went so far as to fight his way through the snow and wind to board a stalled train—the 9:30 a.m. out of Hartford, which he met in its stalled position near Chapel Street in New Haven. The engineer had spent the better part of the day attempting to bust through the tall drifts piled onto the tracks by the driving winds, but he finally had to give in to the elements and work with his conductor to make the passengers comfortable. "General Conductor 'Wat' Ellsworth greeted the reporter with effusiveness," the paper said. "His passengers had been cared for in regal style and been served with refreshments. Later in the day thirty of them set out for the Elliott House. In the drawing room car were Judge E. A. Storrs and party bound for Florida. They remained in the car all night. They were supplied with eatables from the depot restaurant."

Many parents made the decision to keep their children home from school on Monday rather than send them out into the blizzard. Some

People cleared what paths they could through the deep drifts. (Connecticut Historical Society)

did arrive at school and classes began more or less on schedule, but by midday, New Haven school superintendent Dutton communicated with all the schools that it was time to send the children home. "At the high school two boys were sent home with each girl, to see that she got home safely," the newspaper assured its readers. "At the other schools the boys had to see that the girls all got home." Teachers, however, were not so lucky: Many of them decided to wait out the weather, thinking that it could not possibly keep on storming at this rate for much longer. They were sorely mistaken, and most of them found themselves waylaid at the school well into the evening. Some of them finally made their way to "places near the schools" where they could spend the night, though we can guess that others actually spent the night in the school buildings.

The teachers were not the only residents who could not get home Monday night. Most people had reached their places of work on Monday morning, arriving late and covered in snow but making the required effort to put in a full day's business. When the workday ended, however, they found the horsecars stranded and encased in snow, the sidewalks covered in high drifts, and the streets impassable. The young women who worked in shops were excused earlier than normal to give them an opportunity to try to get home, but they were ill-equipped to walk home through so much snow and ice. "It was all a man could do to brave the storm, let alone a woman's trying to overcome it," the *Journal-Courier*'s reporter determined in the quaint thinking of the time. "The girls in the shops in West Haven had to stay there all night. . . . Two girls who had taken refuge at the Selden House attempted to go home about 9 o'clock. They got as far as the corner of Court and State street, and the storm was so blinding that they had to return."

Others tried to find alternatives that simply don't exist in a storm of such magnitude and were met with the opportunism that sometimes emerges during a major emergency. Three men stranded on the Branford train, which had come to rest at the Fair Haven East cut, waited seven hours for the storm to abate and finally decided that they did not want to spend the night there. They tried to hire a carriage and horse to take them the rest of the way home, but no one wanted to venture out with a team in such weather. "No one would bring them over unless they bought the horse," the newspaper said. "This they refused to do, and they started to walk over." The three men finally reached New Haven at about 6:00 p.m., spent and covered in snow after at least two hours of fighting their way through whiteout conditions.

"The storm here is the most horrible ever known," the New Haven news office said in a dispatch to the *Hartford Courant*, the only place still connected by wire, as Monday evening arrived. "Drifts are piled from ten to forty feet high on the sidewalks. . . . Women employed in the large factories did not attempt to reach home but remained all night in the factories . . . Five trains from the north and east are snowbound within the city limits and the passengers have been removed to hotels. . . . The wind is blowing at the rate of 30 miles an hour and men dare not attempt to walk a half dozen blocks from the center of the city. Many business men had not attempted to reach home, but stopped at the hotels, which are crowded to the utmost capacity."

Hartford also maintained contact with Springfield, Massachusetts, where a reporter called the storm "simply unprecedented. The schools were closed for the day and many children were lost in the blinding sleet and awful drifts. But no fatalities are known." Streetcars stood abandoned along their lines, and hundreds of "shop girls and compositors" who could not find a way to get home spent the night at hotels near their places of work. Trains crowded the depot, stranding people for whom Hartford was not their destination. "The hotels about the depot are filled to overflowing with jolly crowds of traveling people who are giving all sorts of entertainments," the *Courant* said. "The Murray & Murphy Company and Hi Henry's Minstrels are among them." Luckily for Springfield, the storm had blown itself out there by Monday evening, though not without exacting its price: the paper reported that a Boston & Albany employee, working to plow a road west of the city, had been killed that afternoon "by his own carelessness in handling the big and freaky lever. It flew up with terrific force, hit him under the chin and broke his neck."

Reports continued to filter in from across the state. Traffic stood still in Meriden, stores remained shuttered, and schools closed early to send children back to their homes before the routes became completely obliterated. Bridgeport closed down its railroad station early, as no train could approach the city and supervisors wisely decided not to send any more locomotives out to become stranded. "Stores are closed and business is generally suspended," the paper informed its readers. Waterbury shut down its shops, schools, and factories and sent all its residents home to wait out the blizzard. Hartford saw some of the worst of the storm, becoming "completely paralyzed," according to the paper. "No casualties, but several narrow escapes from death by exposure are reported. Large manufacturing concerns have quartered their hands in their factories or in neighboring hotels last night." The head of the railroad in Hartford, Superintendent Davidson, told the reporter that in his thirty-one years of railroad service, this was "the worst storm in his experience."

Not everyone suffered significant inconvenience during the storm. In Boston, some of the highest waves ever seen at the Deer Island breakwater entertained onlookers throughout the day as the wind whipped up the surf. "There is great excitement at Crescent Beach," a report out of Boston in the *Hartford Courant* informed readers on Tuesday morning, March 13. "The water covers a portion of the neck and is rapidly rising, and people living near the shore are in alarm from Great Head to Point of Pines. Many people are going to Crescent Beach to witness the unusual sight, and the proprietor of the Columbus house has prepared to entertain a crowd."

At Newport, Rhode Island, waves reported to be "the largest ever seen" eroded the coastline as the snow turned to rain and the wind maintained hurricane speeds. Block Island, off the coast of Rhode Island, took serious damage as waves dispensed with the breakwater and rose to unprecedented levels. "Captain Waters, from the lifesaving station near Newport, says the sea is the worst he has ever experienced," the *Courant* said.

More reports reached the *Courant*'s news desk from towns in Vermont and from New York City, all with the same news: schools and businesses closed, factories and mills gone silent, roads blocked, snowdrifts twenty and thirty feet high, trains at a standstill. A rumor arose from Stamford, Connecticut, that the Western Union telegraph and telephone offices had been destroyed by a fire raging through the city, but this later turned out to be a hoax.

At about 3:00 a.m. Tuesday morning, the wind in Connecticut and Rhode Island subsided and the snowfall ceased. New Haven, Hartford, and all the cities and towns in southern Connecticut and Rhode Island began the long, difficult process of surveying the damage, freeing stranded trains and horsecars, clearing the streets and sidewalks, and returning to the normalcy they had enjoyed just two days earlier.

"SILENCE," proclaimed the headline in the *Boston Globe* on the morning of March 13. It expounded bleakly in a series of subheads:

"The Wires All Down. Many Railway Trains Stalled. Snowed Under on N.E. Roads. Ice Packed Solidly On Tracks. The Western Union Co. in a Bad Fix. News By Long-Distance Telephone Only. Workingman Housed in a Car All Night. Storm-Swept Revere Beach—Great Desolation. Cottages Destroyed and Bulkheads Wrecked. Two Holyoke Factories Crushed in by the Weight of Snow. South Shore Seas Sweeping Over Minot's."

And these were just the headlines.

The *Globe* took a moment to remind readers of its dedication: "People must have the news, and when there is news The Globe, with its superb facilities, is always ready to spread it before the people." The writer, who may well have spent the night at the newspaper fielding what calls could get through, continued with poetic flair: "The long distance telephone refused to be downed by old Boreas [Greek god of the north wind], who went on a spree yesterday and amused himself by indulging in a lot of malicious mischief. He blew upon the telegraph wires and they went down like grain before the reaper's blade; he nodded to the local telephone wires and they sank to earth. But when he tackled the new copper wires of the New England Long Distance Telephone he found he had quite a contract on his hands to knock them out."

Thanks to this new service and the dedicated long-distance telephone in the newsroom, the *Globe* continued to communicate with the Associated Press and newspapers in New York, Albany, Springfield, Worcester, New Haven, Hartford, and Providence throughout the storm. The collected reports revealed devastation across the region. On the Boston coast, railroad tracks were encased in ice and cottages had been ripped to pieces by the wind, now standing deep in the debris from patios, gardens, and piazzas. Rocks, trash, and the remains of various buildings lay across roads, all gathered and dumped there by the massive waves breaking over the shoreline. Seawater flooded cross streets, and sand and gravel piled up alongside the snow. One huge wave lifted the bulkhead in front of the Hotel Shirley and tossed it across the road and over a cottage—and once the bulkhead was gone, the waves disassembled the road and washed it away, eroding the cliff and undermining the stability of cottages that sat atop it.

The grand sight at Crescent Beach of the waves at high tide quickly became something of a nightmare as breakers came in farther than ever

Stores on streets in Connecticut cities nearly vanished behind massive snowbanks. (Connecticut Historical Society)

before, washing away the tracks of the Boston, Revere Beach & Lynn Railroad. Railroad workers had predicted the danger earlier, moving two trains back and away from the ocean's edge just before the tracks became submerged in seawater and crumbled into the surf. Mrs. John T. Gallagher, a resident of one of the nearby cottages, earned her place in blizzard history by serving the train's stranded passengers coffee from her own home as they waited to be evacuated.

The report from Providence contained more word of snowbound trains and passengers, some of which had clearly been trapped since early Monday. "The 4 o'clock Worcester train of yesterday has not reached here yet, and it is supposed to be stuck in the snow drifts north of Woonsocket," the reporter told the *Globe*. "North of the Rhode Island line there is no travel on the road whatever, and several trains are reported stalled on the Worcester road. The New York & New England brought two locomotives and a single car from the little village of Washington, 18 miles from here, requiring two hours to make the trip." A train with two full carloads of workers trying to get home remained stranded somewhere near Springfield, with no further word on their condition or their ability to stay warm or get food. Horsecar routes within the city were no better. "Six and eight horses are used on a car," the reporter noted, where one or two would be ample in normal weather. "There is a foot of snow on the level, half of it being solid ice and sleet."

Even worse for Providence, the temperature had begun to drop, causing the sleet and snow to freeze solid and turn the roads into frictionless slides. The newspaper office received word that a train that had left the city Monday night had managed to reach Oakland, Rhode Island, "after a most terrible experience, the passengers suffering from lack of fire and food." The fact that there was any word of a train's whereabouts became an anomaly, however, as most trains stranded in deep snow could not communicate with the railroad stations, leaving them to fend for themselves amid the solid ice and sleet.

The railroads moved quickly to organize large work details, sending gangs of men with shovels and ice breaking equipment to begin to free the tracks and bring the icebound travelers into the stations. Many sections of track required repairs as well as snow removal, however, and "the progress of repairing them will be very slow, as the absence of railway traffic makes the task a herculean one," the Providence reporter confirmed.

With no trains, delivery of mail from New York and Boston ceased, and newspaper distribution outside the cities ground to a halt as well. This did not stop editors and reporters from churning out papers, however, and those in central locations with working telephone service maintained communication with every community they could, leaving us a dramatic and detailed record of events that otherwise would be lost to history.

In Cambridge, Massachusetts, for example, a fire broke out on Monday night in the cellar of Samuel McIntire's grocery story, positioned in a one-story block on Main Street, opposite the city hall. Several other shops shared the building, including a millinery shop owned by Amelia J. La Breque, L. B. Chandler's provision store, and the E. A. Green & Co. hardware store. A police patrolman named Hiscock spotted smoke coming from the building and went closer to investigate, most likely seeing the flames through a basement window. He moved quickly to the nearest emergency call box—number 36—a few hundred yards away at the corner, but when he pulled the handle, the ice-covered box malfunctioned and tapped out the wrong position number to the fire department. "At North Cambridge it rung 16, while at East Cambridge the number given was 62," the *Globe* explained. "At Harvard Square the number of the box was sounded properly on the first sound, but it took the rest of the night to give the three other sounds. At the Port the box didn't ring at all."

Dodging snowdrifts and icy patches, Hiscock ran to the nearest firehouse and alerted the men there, and barely took time to catch his breath before he hurried off to the police station. There the officers on duty sent a messenger to the home of one Dr. Litchfield, a clergyman, where the runner rang the doorbell again and again until the man answered. He urged the pastor to go to his place of worship, the Universalist church in the same area as the fire, and ring the bell to alert firefighters and other citizens throughout Cambridge to the additional emergency in progress. The plea worked; the pastor rushed to the church and rang the bell, bringing in the fire brigade.

In the heavy snow and towering drifts, methods for extinguishing the flames "revived old fire days," the *Boston Globe* said. With the usual water sources buried in snowbanks, those fighting the blaze may have resorted to passing buckets of water hand-over-hand and other activities long since abandoned by professionals. They succeeded in stopping the fire before it spread to other buildings, but the stores in the block took on significant water and smoke damage—up to $12,000 in total, the paper said, adding, "There is partial insurance on the whole."

The *Globe* also carried a story about a "disastrous fire" in a town it reported as Phoenix, Rhode Island (which may have been Phenix Village), which consumed the showroom and warehouse of J. T. Arnold, an undertaker and furniture dealer, as well as the adjacent railroad depot, the home of the Selloway family, and the offices of McGregor G. A. R. Post. The entire fifty-by-fifty-foot building known as the Mumford block fell to the flames, while firefighters battled the continued snow and sleet in a valiant but futile attempt to gain control of the blaze. "The Selloway family, composed of five persons, barely escaped with their lives," the paper said. "Only a trunk was saved from their household effects."

It took hundreds of workmen and many private citizens days to clear the streets enough for commerce and traffic to resume. (Connecticut Historical Society)

By Wednesday, March 14, as people dug out of their immediate surroundings, recovery efforts redoubled across southern New England. News from New York City remained grim, with hundreds of lives lost, people displaced, trains derailed, ships and fishing vessels wrecked, and estimates that wire services would take days or longer to repair. The *Fall River Daily Evening News* reported Wednesday night, however, that trains from the north and east had begun to arrive at Framingham, outside of Boston, though trains from the south and west continued to languish as large crews dug day and night to free them. Word of fatalities in New England began to reach the papers: an engineer died on the Fitchburg road when two snowplows collided; a track walker was killed by a plow at the Hoosic tunnel; and a man wandered off the road in Adams and died of exposure.

Prospects remained dismal in New Haven as the full impact of the blizzard became more and more apparent. Residents accustomed to buying fresh food daily at local markets found that there were no provisions to be had. "It is believed that there is not more than 36 hours' ordinary food supply in the city," the *Globe* reported on the morning of March 14. "Today they began to buy for a week or a fortnight at least, as there is no chance of getting beef or meat coming from New

York or the West. Most of the groceries are cleaned out, and there is hardly a loaf of bread for sale tonight." People also began buying coal "by the hodful, and drawing it to their homes on handsleds," for fear that this basic heating supply would run out as well. Already the New Haven Hotel and the Elliott House, stuffed to capacity with stranded rail passengers, had run out of coal and saw their food supplies dwindling. As many as twenty-six trains waited in New Haven to proceed to their original destinations, leaving hundreds of passengers stranded and requiring sustenance and warmth. "[Railroad] Vice President Reed says that if he had 5000 shovelers he could not do anything toward getting the trains underway," the paper said. "There are trains on the shoreline that have not been heard from since yesterday noon."

Hartford's report to the *Globe* said that business and transportation were at a standstill there as well, although "grocery stores, markets and saloons" had managed to open their doors and welcome whatever customers could reach them. "The horse railroad company has broken a way through Main Street and will begin running sleighs in the morning, it being impossible to run any cars," its report continued. It also told of a fire in a barn Tuesday night, near the Union railroad depot. "None of the steamers could be used, and the firemen were obliged to carry their hose in various ways. One company dragged a rowboat, another a large sleigh, and still another carried hose on the shoulders of the men. They succeeded in extinguishing the fire with water from the hydrants."

Reports began to come in about train cars filled with passengers that had been stranded in the snow and cold for thirty-six hours or more, some with no access to food. A train stalled at Berlin happened to be carrying fresh meat in a freight car, so passengers raided the car and took what they needed to survive.

News out of Meriden made it clear that the gangs of men shoveling in the cold knew full well their value to the railroads. Some two hundred men staged a strike on the tracks on Tuesday afternoon, demanding as much as fifty cents an hour more than they were being paid for the backbreaking work. "They were retained," the news item concluded, demonstrating that the railroad also realized that there could be no recovery effort without this crew.

All along the Connecticut and Rhode Island seaboard, the great shovel-out went on for days, until finally, by the following Monday, most transportation and commerce had resumed. Telegraph lines reopened as crews in New York City and beyond reerected poles and untangled wires. The nation's largest metropolis had taken the brunt of the storm, but the people of New England would not soon forget the magnitude of the damage, the isolation caused by downed communication systems, and the potential for exposure and starvation they had faced. For the first time, utilities understood the precarious nature of their services if snow and ice could paralyze them overnight, and plans began to bury at least some cables underground to avoid such a catastrophe in the future. The blizzard of 1888 underscored the fragility of modern life against the power of nature's forces, leaving officials and average citizens with an uneasy understanding of the need to protect themselves against the next major disaster.

## CHAPTER NINE

# "No Hope for Relief"— The Heat Wave of 1911

I magine if July temperatures in New England could soar to the kinds of highs people expect in Texas or Arizona: well over one hundred degrees every day for more than a week. How would lifelong New Englanders cope with such a heat wave?

In an area utterly unaccustomed to this level of summer heat, people might not realize the kind of toll such oppressive weather can take on the body's ability to cope. Leaving the house could mean exposure to baking sun, sizzling sidewalks, and road tar that liquefies and squishes underfoot. The air feels thick and retains industrial pollutants, making it difficult to breathe. The heat robs people of energy, reducing productivity and making even a casual walk seem like a chore. Animals begin to drop in their tracks. Beaches and lakeshores become overcrowded with bathers seeking relief.

Imagine enduring all this before the invention of air conditioning.

Just such a heat wave parked itself in New England in the summer of 1911, long before people walked the streets comfortably in sleeveless shirts, crop tops, or shorts. It trapped men swathed in business suits of long pants, coat, vest, shirt buttoned to the neck, and tie, and women in Edwardian-style dresses with long skirts, long sleeves, and high necks— women who were cinched into tight corsets to achieve the required tiny waist and slim hips. With no cooling systems to regulate indoor temperatures, the heat became inescapable, a stifling force that imprisoned workplaces and sent sleepless citizens to their roofs and backyards in the middle of the night in hopes of finding even the slightest breeze. Worse, it became a killer, bending the weakest residents to its will and robbing them of their last breath. No weather event in New England's

Men wore many layers of clothing every day in 1911, even in the heat of summer. (Courtesy Library of Congress)

recorded history can take responsibility for as many human deaths as the heat wave of 1911.

The product of a hot, dry weather system out of the southern Great Plains, the heat wave arrived on July 3 on a strong, stifling wind, so powerful that it dominated all the region's cooling ocean breezes, blowing them back out to sea. New Englanders expected the usual afternoon thunderstorm to wash away this sudden torrid spell, but no rain came—in fact, temperatures continued to climb throughout the day, reaching ninety-six degrees in Hartford, Connecticut, before noon and rising eleven degrees in half an hour in Providence, Rhode Island.

Readers of the *Bridgeport Times and Evening Farmer* on July 5 learned that Monday, July 3, was the hottest day in the history of the Connecticut city. The mercury in weather observer William Jennings's thermometer reached 101 degrees at 2:00 p.m. that day, surpassing the previous record of 100 degrees on July 2, 1891. While Jennings did not spot such a height in Bridgeport again as the heat wave progressed, temperatures remained in the high 90s on Tuesday and Wednesday, taxing the city's electricity supply as people ran every fan they could find in an attempt to beat the heat. Down the road in Hartford, the heat increased on July 5, sending the mercury over the 100 degree mark for the first time in recorded history.

"There was much suffering in this city during the day," the *Hartford Courant* told its readers. "The temperature on the street reached 104½. . . . Three persons are dead as a result of the heat, which was made the more unendurable by high humidity. There were a large number of prostrations," the word the media used to describe people fainting and being rushed to hospitals. Meanwhile, a massive rainstorm—"one of the most terrific thunderstorms which has been known for many years," according to the *Courant*—came to the Connecticut River valley in Massachusetts near Springfield, dumping 5.65 inches of rain on the area and washing out the Boston & Maine railroad line north of Holyoke.

By the end of the first uncomfortable day, the *Boston Globe* reported that the heat wave extended all the way to Chicago and south to Baltimore, with a high of 104 in Lancaster, Pennsylvania, and 107 in Washington, DC, for the annual Independence Day celebration. "A Fourth of July more oppressive and sweltering than any for a decade past is the prophecy made by weather bureau officials tonight after a careful study of the weather map," the *Globe's* Washington bureau reported on July 4. "With reports of temperatures of 104 degrees in four widely separated cities, and 20 other cities broiling in a temperature of 100 or higher, no hope for relief could be discovered."

Not surprisingly, eleven people suffering from heat exhaustion in Hartford alone had to be taken to hospitals by ambulance on July 5, "and the ambulance men at police headquarters handled so many that several times they felt like staying in the hospital for an ice bath themselves," the *Courant* reported. "About the time the ambulance would get backed into the police garage, the bell would ring again."

Reports came in from all over the eastern half of the country, listing the names and circumstances of the dead. On the first day of the heat wave, fourteen people died in New York City, another fourteen in Chicago, twelve in Pittsburgh, more than twenty in Philadelphia, four in Baltimore, and eight in St. Louis. The roles of those who fainted in the streets or were carried prostrate out of their homes climbed as well, doubling and tripling the number of casualties in each major city.

The heat soared to 104 degrees in Haverhill, Massachusetts, where young John J. McCarthy, just thirty-one years old, was discovered dead in his room at a lodging house on Locke Street at the end of the day. "It is not known when McCarthy went to his room, but as he had not been seen all day, other lodgers visited his room and found him dead," the *Globe* reported. The medical examiner said McCarthy had been dead about five hours when his fellow lodgers found him. Another man, Freeman Shugrue, collapsed on the sidewalk on Washington Street in Haverhill, and languished in the hospital in serious condition at the paper's press time. Doctors and nurses who rarely saw cases of heat exhaustion struggled to keep up with the mounting volume of patients, while word flew from one place of business to the next that employees simply could not tolerate the internal temperatures of office buildings and factories. Those whose work required them to be outdoors received orders to pack up and go home. "Street laborers on Main st were obliged to quit this morning, while the street railways, which are repairing their tracks, laid their men off," the *Globe* noted.

Down the road in Cambridge, Mayor Barry ordered the fire department to open hydrants and flood parts of East Cambridge at the request of the area's alderman, James F. Black. "Practically all of the factories in the . . . East Cambridge district closed down for the afternoon and many private business houses as well," the *Globe* said. "Hundreds slept in the open last night." The news from Cambridge contained the names of several women who had lost consciousness in the streets and been rushed to hospitals or revived at the nearby Kidder's drug store.

Large animal veterinarians had their hands full, as horses suffered just as much as humans in the heat. The *Courant* described the plight of a horse that pulled wagons for the Thomas Stafford construction company, which collapsed in a gutter just off Main Street in the middle of the afternoon. "Loads of ice were dumped in the street, packed about the animal's body in blankets, and a line of hose was run out . . . and a stream of cold water was kept playing on the animal," the paper reported. The doctor managed to have the horse moved to its stable early in the evening, but it died later that night. A second horse owned by the Stafford company was stricken later the same afternoon and died around midnight.

Women's fashions required tight corsets and long skirts at any time of year. (Courtesy Library of Congress)

By the morning of July 4, the heat in New England had become national news. The *Salt Lake Telegram* in Utah told its readers that Concord, New Hampshire, had been the hottest place in the United States at 8:00 a.m. on July 3, with the mercury registering ninety-nine degrees. The *Cincinnati Inquirer* carried news of northern heat as well: "The White Mountains of New Hampshire, famed for their cooling breezes, offered little relief, for at some points the mercury registered 96 in the shade," it claimed. "At Burlington, Vt., the Weather Bureau reported a temperature of 100, exceeding by four degrees the highest mark reached during the 70 years that local records have been kept."

People freed from their workplaces by either heat or the holiday leapt into whatever pond, creek, or bay they could reach in the hope of

Children licking a block of ice on a busy street get some relief from days of stifling heat. (Courtesy Library of Congress)

cooling down, underestimating the depth of the water or the shock of the cold on their overheated bodies. Of those who attempted to escape the heat by bathing in one of the region's many rivers, twelve lost their lives on July 3, creating an additional spike in the death toll. The fact that all these drowning victims were in their twenties or younger simply piled tragedy on tragedy as the first day of the cloying heat came to a close.

Fourteen-year-old Mary Doyle of North Brighton and her two friends, fifteen-year-old Sarah E. Gaudett and Annie H. White, waded out from the "dike"—a small beach area on the Charles River—toward the channel, where the water becomes deeper fairly suddenly. In water up to her neck, Annie began to panic, and the other two girls realized she did not know how to swim. Sarah became frightened, and in a moment, she was swallowing water and could not move out of the deeper spot on her own. The terrified young women grabbed onto Mary's clothing and nearly dragged her down with them as she did her best to swim to shallower water.

"Mary backed away, watching a convenient opportunity of getting at the other girls in such a way as not to be hampered herself," the *Globe* said. Sarah and Annie kept trying to grab for a lifesaving hold, however, until they pulled her under and into the same trouble they were attempting to escape.

Meanwhile, nearly one hundred other girls watched from the safety of the shore. Only Mary's cousin Ellen Maher leapt into the water and swam out to Mary, gaining enough of a grip on her to drag her to shore. Annie and Sarah were not so lucky. They both perished in the water, unable to get firm footing or to swim the short distance to the shallower water.

Reports came from Waterbury, Connecticut, that four people had died of heat prostration on July 5, including a seven-month-old baby girl. The July 6 *Norwich Bulletin*, also in Connecticut, carried a report from Boston that a total of fifty-seven people throughout New England had died in heat-related afflictions, most from heat prostration, but others from unique accidents: John Merle of Hartford climbed onto the roof of his house to sleep in an attempt to escape the heat, but he rolled off and fell four stories to the concrete below.

"The prostrations ran into the hundreds," the Boston report continued. "The usual number of drownings which follow in the wake of hot days also resulted, half a dozen being reported."

The list of those who died in the persistent heat grew longer with each hour of temperatures in the nineties and above. Elderly people were discovered dead in their beds after a sweltering night aggravated a heart condition. Babies too young to regulate their own body temperature succumbed to days of being much too warm. A sixty-two-year-old undertaker in Hudson, Massachusetts, dropped dead of heat-related heart failure while preparing a body for a funeral. Three people died in Fitchburg on July 5, and one perished in Brockton while a dozen more were rushed to hospitals when they lost consciousness in the streets or at work. A Brockton shoe factory with more than one thousand employees shut down at noon on July 6 when the heat on the factory floor became dangerously high.

On Thursday, July 6, with the heat wave officially completing its fifth day, the *Fall River Daily Evening News* promised relief by the following morning. It made this cheery prediction based on the knowledge of a Boston weather forecaster named Smith, who saw the potential for a drop of as much as twenty degrees by Friday morning, the newspaper said. Thursday, however, had been another scorcher. "This section of New England to-day again began to wilt under a death-dealing temperature and a high humidity," the reporter wrote. "The blistering sun again shone down from a clear sky. . . . Prostrations were numerous on the streets and in workshops and offices. The infant mortality continued to be appalling. People in the crowded tenements were getting frantic." By the end of the day, New England added sixty-two deaths to the weather's toll, and Boston alone saw twenty-six additional cases of people dropping in the streets or fainting in their homes or workplaces. "The prostrations have been so numerous that the staffs of the city hospitals have been unable to record the names of the victims, and any estimate of their number is purely conjectural," the *Washington Post* added in its report on Boston.

Providence reported seven new deaths on July 6, in part because of a shift in the wind that sent the cooling ocean breezes packing as southwest winds carried in even hotter air than before. As the mercury soared, "the activity of the hospital ambulance corps continued," the newspaper said. "The toll of the heat wave of the past five days in this state up to noon today was 12 deaths and more than 50 prostrations, the great majority of which were in this city."

In this era before refrigerators, the fifth day of the intense heat led to a shortage of manufactured ice, leaving homemakers and businesses with no ability to keep raw meat, milk, and other products from spoiling. Milk also became a premium product, with people consuming more milk than normal in an effort to quench thirst in the heat. One horse pulling a milk wagon lost its composure and attempted to bolt, dragging a police patrolman thirty-five feet as he attempted to catch and calm the creature. Patrolman Trainor was "severely crushed" by the animal and had to be hospitalized.

City and town officials across the region began to look for ways to bring their citizens some relief. Boston mayor Patrick A. Collins asked the city's ferry services to offer free excursions for tenement dwellers and others among the poor. "During the afternoon [of July 6], word was passed around that all who desired it might sleep on the Common," the Fall River paper reported. "The result was that this breathing spot of the city resembled a huge dormitory. Whole families were camped out under the trees." The city estimated that some two thousand people took Boston up on its offer and slept outdoors on the Common that night, giving the fire department the opportunity to flush the streets of the tenement district with water from the hydrants overnight, with the dual purpose of cooling those who stayed behind and removing the stench of waste decomposing in the blistering heat.

Reports from Lowell, Massachusetts, indicated that the city had just about run out of water in its main reservoir. Residents desperate to beat the heat drank much more water than usual and bathed in cooling water more often, consuming two million gallons a day more than normal and leaving the city's water pumps struggling to keep up with the demand. The water board put out a bulletin warning people to limit their use of this basic necessity or risk having no water at all. "People in Lowell were using water with the greatest care to-day, fearing a water famine," the newspapers said.

In the town of Webster, Massachusetts, a theatrical troupe performing a melodrama during the hottest part of the day succumbed to the additional heat generated by the lighting and stifling theater. Some of them collapsed onstage, and all members of the troupe ended up in the hospital before the day was out, where they were expected to recover from heat exhaustion. Factories in Wakefield, Massachusetts, shut their doors on Thursday and sent their one thousand workers home after one, Patrick Walsh, lost consciousness in the heat on a factory floor. The iron foundry at Whitins Machine shops in Whitinsville became unbearably overheated with temperatures sending the mercury above 120 degrees, dropping five of the 2,500 employees to the floor, and threatening additional casualties. The foremen had no choice but to close up shop until the weather cooled.

Holidaysburg saw one of the worst consequences of the heat wave, when a massive, unscheduled detonation at the Standard Powder Works explosives manufacturing facility appeared to be set off by intense heat. Four men in the powder works died in the blast, which took place at Horrell Station on the Petersburg branch of the Pennsylvania railroad. "The storage house, containing tons of dynamite, nitroglycerine, and powder, was the only building saved," the report said.

Rutland, Vermont, reported an astonishing 102 degrees on July 6, but its *Daily Herald* managed to dish out some sass on the fifth day of the weather event. "Residents of these United States have been wont to boast of their peculiar sections as being cool in summer and warm in winter," it said, essentially summing up the benefits of living in Vermont's Green Mountains. "They have imposed upon the credulity of a long-suffering and good-natured people for many years, but they have met their Nemesis. Their wordy vaunts have given place to solemn facts registered by the thermometer. Rutland herself, a mountain resort, is willing to swap weather with someplace else and take a chance on getting something different from what she has."

As New England festered, however, the rest of the country began to see significant relief. Forecasters in Washington, DC, boldly predicted that the North Atlantic states would finally cool down throughout the day on July 7, seeing refreshing temperatures in the sixties and seventies by that evening. New York City had begun the day on Thursday at a pleasant seventy-four degrees, and Washington itself enjoyed an eighty-degree day. New England contained three of the four hottest spots in the nation on Thursday—Boston; Northfield, Vermont; and Concord, New Hampshire (the fourth was Syracuse, New York)—so this faint ray of hope for an end to the region's suffering buoyed spirits as another sweaty night led to the sixth torrid morning in a row.

On July 6, thunderstorms arrived in parts of the region, even as Providence experienced the hottest day in its history with the mercury reaching 96.6 degrees. Even Portland, Maine, saw the staggeringly high temperature of 97.5, coupled with high humidity that made the atmosphere virtually unbearable inside and out. In Boston, the high reached 103, just a degree short of its July 4 record breaker. On the western edge of New England, meanwhile, evening brought high winds and thundershowers and soaked parts of Connecticut and Burlington, Vermont, but the *Norwich Bulletin* reported on July 7 that after the short relief, it was "warmer than before."

Worse, the thunderstorms knocked out telephone and telegraph lines and flattened crops, particularly in Rutland. Here the rain arrived at 1:30 p.m. and swept through the countryside in successive storms until the last one let up around 5:00 p.m. Lightning strikes sparked

In New York City, children gathered in Madison Square Park to cool off in the fountain. (Courtesy Library of Congress)

fires in farm buildings and in fifteen houses, keeping fire companies racing from one to the next in a steady but often fruitless effort to extinguish the blazes. "The fire alarm wires were out of commission and early in the afternoon many alarms were sent in by automobile, teams and individuals," a special report from Rutland to the *Burlington Free Press* tells us. "Lightning struck the House of Correction and two prisoners were knocked unconscious. Fallen wires blocked the streets in many places and men were stationed at the corners to warn people of danger."

Maine's Somerset and Penobscot counties saw widespread damage to crops and uprooted orchards in the wind and rain, and in Brookfield, Massachusetts, the Unitarian church took a lightning strike that set it ablaze, causing $40,000 in damage. A grain mill and box factory in Wakefield burned and ignited an entire block, including the armory manned by the Sixth Massachusetts Volunteers—which then spread to town hall and half a dozen homes.

All in all, however, the storms did bring some relief from the heat, and July 7 dawned with milder temperatures in the seventies in

Keeping horses cool became a dire necessity during the heat wave. (Courtesy Library of Congress)

communities throughout New England. Winds shifted along the Atlantic coast, bringing in fresh northeasterly breezes off the ocean that rose to twelve miles per hour, clearing the heat and humidity out of homes, apartments, offices, and factories. It seemed that the wave of deadly heat might finally be over.

While heat doesn't leave the kind of devastation in its wake that New Englanders knew from hurricanes and blizzards, it certainly had made its mark on the region as the single deadliest natural phenomenon in New England's history. In the ensuing days, funeral directors in Boston and throughout the northeastern states faced a challenge they had never experienced before: a shortage of traditional carriages and horses to transport so many bodies from homes and hospitals to their facilities for preparation, and then to cemeteries.

"An idea of the large number of deaths was given in last night's edition of the Globe, when there were four columns of death notices, the largest number in the history of any Boston newspaper," the *Globe* said on July 8. "There were notices of 169 deaths, and when it is considered that hearses and carriages are required for each, one can easily see that a problem faces the men who care for the dead."

People attending so many funerals found themselves scrambling for transportation as well. Horses had succumbed to the heat at similar rates to humans, so even when carriages or horse-drawn cars were available, the horses to pull them were not—and the hearses took priority over the mourners' carriages in accessing what horses could be found. Some stable keepers would not rent their horses and hacks to families who had a long way to travel, for fear that animals weakened by the recent heat would drop in their tracks. Families turned to the less familiar option of automobiles to get to cemeteries, calling taxis or using their own vehicles. This signaled a major shift in the way funeral processions had looked for centuries.

"South Boston, famous for its large funerals, severely felt the scarcity of hacks and hearses," the *Globe* said. "The undertakers there had a difficult proposition to provide for the burials. Everywhere a hearse could be secured, it was called for, and many of the undertakers used hearses brought in from out of town. . . . Undertakers within a radius of 25 miles of Boston, having no funerals to care for, found no trouble in getting a good price for the use of their hearses."

In this still-steamy summer week, the motorized vehicle proved its value over much more vulnerable horses, as funeral directors had no choice but to allow automobiles to join corteges. Fears that speedy autos would overtake and harass horse-drawn wagons soon dropped away, with drivers making it clear that they could control their speeds and be courteous to fellow mourners, as well as respecting the vehicle that bore the body.

At last, after a week of oppressive heat, it looked like the "hot wave" had come to an end. July 8 brought "an ideal summer day," the *Globe* reported, with dawn's temperature a cool seventy-one degrees and light breezes pushing the humidity out of the cities. The death toll continued to mount, however, with people who had been stricken by the heat perishing in hospitals or in their own beds as their families struggled to care for them. Months would go by before officials across the region could total all the deaths and quantify those who truly died from heat-related afflictions; in the end, the numbers became murky, but consensus suggested that as many as six hundred people in New England may have been victims of the heat. The eastern half of the nation mourned more than two thousand deaths that week.

Not until 1925 did air conditioners become available, when the public first experienced Willis Carrier's revolutionary centrifugal chiller. Movie theater owners were the first to see the advantages, turning cinemas into the havens of choice for people desperate to beat the summer heat and enjoy a double feature at the same time.

## CHAPTER TEN

# "Tidal Wave of Death"— The Great Boston Molasses Flood of 1919

At about 12:30 p.m. on a mild January afternoon in 1919, patrolman Frank McManus of the Hanover Street police station in downtown Boston stopped at a police signal call box on Commercial Street to make a duty call. As he rang in, he heard a series of ominous rumbling sounds he'd never heard in the years he'd walked this beat: the grinding of metal against metal, the groan of iron forced into bending by tremendous power behind it.

He looked up just in time to see the conical top of a fifty-foot-tall iron tank at 529 Commercial Street slide off and a dark, fragrant liquid begin to flow out —a mass of thick, viscous fluid he had never seen in such a state before. Patrolman McManus recognized the tank as the property of the Purity Distilling Company, makers of alcohol for the United States Industrial Alcohol Company (USIA) for smokeless powder used as a propellant in military weaponry.

In seconds he realized what he saw: the 2.3 million-gallon tank, filled nearly to capacity with molasses. The sweet, sticky stuff poured out of the bursting receptacle at a speed that would most certainly put anyone nearby in immediate danger.

"Those who were in the vicinity at the time said that there was not the usual great detonation accompanying such blasts, but rather a low, rumbling sound more like a quake than otherwise," the *Boston Globe* reported later that afternoon. "The explosion came without the slightest warning. . . . Once the low, rumbling sound was heard no one had a chance to escape. The buildings seemed to cringe up as though they were made of pasteboard."

Before McManus's eyes, a moving black wall more than twenty feet high engulfed and collapsed buildings in its path, spreading in every direction and pouring down the streets and over curbs. He came to his senses and telephoned his station to send every ambulance and police officer to Commercial Street, telling them that loss of lives seemed inevitable.

Structures filled with working people toppled as the molasses swept through, trapping anyone inside under piles of timbers and plaster debris. People who happened to be walking along Commercial Street at the moment the tank ripped open found themselves airborne, lifted off their feet by the rush of air as the tank's cast-iron wall sent a shock wave of wind down the sidewalk. Others had no chance of getting out of the way of the molasses wave and were buried a split second. An entire truck sailed through the air and landed across the road from its original location, mangled by the impact.

The sticky fluid piled up against curbs and quickly flowed over and beyond them, covering everything within two blocks of the tank in every direction.

Buildings came loose from their foundations and became flotsam in the gluey mire. Purity Distilling's plant and offices went down instantly, the people inside shouting for help as molasses and wreckage buried them alive. The dark-brown tide completely wrecked the Public Works Department, carrying its buildings down the road and depositing them in North End Park, some one hundred feet away. The structures crumpled and came apart before they found a resting place in the center of the park, giving nine of the fifteen people inside a moment's chance to escape with their lives. Falling walls and beams crushed the other six people.

"Unlike an ocean wave, whose momentum is concentrated in one direction, the wall of molasses pushed in all directions after it escaped the confines of the tank, so that it was more like four *separate* walls of viscous liquid smashing across the wharf and into the street," wrote journalist and author Stephen Puleo in his thrilling and thorough book, *Dark Tide: The Great Boston Molasses Flood of 1919.* "Add to that the

Entire buildings succumbed to the molasses as it flowed from the busted tank on Commercial Street in Boston. (Courtesy Library of Congress)

speed with which the molasses traveled—thirty-five miles per hour initially—the fact that the tank itself disintegrated into deadly steel missiles, and that thousands of fastening rivets turned into lethal steel bullets, and the result was destruction in a congested area equal to that of even the worst natural disaster."

Employees of the Paving Department sat eating their lunches when the wave of molasses hit their building without a moment's warning, shoving the walls over and onto the workers and releasing girders down onto their heads. No one came out of the demolished structure unscathed, but some did survive, albeit with significant injuries. The men on duty on fireboat Engine 31, docked next to its building, watched the building collapse but escaped relatively unhurt—so they were ready to join the rescue effort, alerting Boston's fire headquarters to the disaster and making their way ashore to help.

Police and firemen arriving on the scene struggled even to approach the destroyed buildings, wading through the thick, inky fluid, and following the sounds of people calling for help. "Some of the people who had been caught in the debris were frightfully hurt, the injuries causing them to shriek at every move and these shouts were not quieted when they were placed in the ambulances," the *Globe*'s reporter wrote, clearly as an eyewitness to the event. "Altogether it was an agonizing quarter or half an hour that the rescuers endured, but they worked heroically, and by 1 p.m. it was estimated between 100 and 150 persons had been taken from the ruins and hurried away to hospitals or had been treated by physicians in the neighborhood."

Horses pulling cars in the streets or stabled at the Public Works department perished under the rain of debris, while others sustained injuries so grave that police made the painful decision to shoot them on the spot, rather than allowing them to suffer. One horse and its driver near the molasses tank were entirely submerged in the stuff, but they struggled their way out and managed to escape. They "crawled out and hurried away from the scene," the *Globe* reported.

Above the surface of the wharf, an elevated train bound for the North Station came to a halt at North End Park as the tank began to disgorge its contents. The engineer, seeing that something was terribly amiss up ahead, managed to bring the train to a stop and threw it into reverse. His quick thinking saved the train and everyone on board, as a section of the L structure ended up in ruins and stymied continued traffic on the elevated railway. "The forward trucks of the first car were lifted completely off the rails and set down on the ties," the *Globe* reported. Had the train continued forward, it would have been knocked off the tracks and thrown to the pavement, an accident that would have injured or killed dozens of people.

Lieutenant Commander Howard G. Copeland, in charge of the Navy's ship USS *Nantucket* docked at the North End pier, saw the tank come apart and ordered his full complement of sailors ashore to help. He led 116 men off the ship at double-quick time and began the kind of rescue operation for which the sailors were trained, stationing some as patrols to keep people away from the quagmire, and sending others to attempt to find living people or bodies in the building wreckage. Soon the sailors were covered in copper-colored molasses. They did "admirable and heroic rescue work," the *Globe* noted the following day, discovering the bodies of six men crushed by beams as the office buildings crumbled, and another twenty people or more who were injured but alive. The sailors carried the injured out of the muck on stretchers and brought them to park benches to await the ambulances already on their way. The men of the USS *Bessie J*, an ammunition lighter also docked in the harbor, also left their ship as soon as they saw the disaster begin to unfold and were soon "wallowing knee deep with civilians in the flood of molasses, rescuing the injured and the bodies of the dead," the *Globe* said.

At 521 Commercial Street, two elderly women made their home in a small apartment. Mrs. Elizabeth O'Brien and her sister, Mrs. Mary Keenan, were at home to hear the low rumble and feel the impact of the initial rush of air as the molasses tank came apart. In seconds, their building began to move—not shake as if in an earthquake, but actually sail across the road and into North End Park with them inside, "midst a roar of crashing timbers and a deluge of seething molasses," the *Globe* said the following day. Miraculously, the roof and floor did not collapse, keeping the women well above the sticky black liquid that pulled so many others down into its grasp. Soon the men of the *Nantucket* reached the partially upright building and heard cries coming from a dormer on the upper floor, and realized that someone had survived and needed help to get out. They entered the house and found Mrs. O'Brien injured and Mrs. Keenan unhurt, but once they got the two women outside, Mrs. Keenan promptly fainted. The sailors brought Mrs. Keenan to a waiting ambulance and saw her whisked away to a hospital, while Mrs. O'Brien received first aid in the brick house at the far end of the park until her son arrived, collected her, and drove her to a hospital as well.

"Within a short time every Police Department ambulance, those from the various hospitals, Health Department, the Metropolitan Chapter of the Red Cross, the United States Army and the United States Navy and a detail from General Hospital No. 10 of the Department of the Northeast were on the scene and busy ministering to and carrying away the injured," the *Globe* said. Police officials arrived as well, as did Walter Wedger, an explosives expert for the state police, and medical examiner George B. McGrath.

Elevated train structure is a twisted mass of metal on Atlantic Avenue. (Courtesy *Boston Globe* via Getty Images)

The first ambulance on the scene had Red Cross Ambulance Corps commander Mrs. Carlisle Emery at the wheel, and she lost no time in coordinating the first evacuations and supervising more than twenty female ambulance drivers and nurses at her command. Soon Mrs. James Lawrence Jr., head of the Red Cross Canteen, joined her with her own team of assistants, and they made gallons of coffee and distributed it and many plates of fresh doughnuts to the fire crew and others working in the rescue operation. The women began their task by wading through the sticky morass to reach the firemen, police, and sailors hard at work there, but before very long, police superintendent Michael H. Crowley saw them struggling against the brown tide and made arrangements with the parks department for a large room in which they could set up their refreshments and keep them coming without endangering themselves. "A number of young women stayed on the job all night, serving the 30 detailed firemen and other workers with hot coffee and lunches," the *Globe* reported.

So many first responders arrived, in fact, that within an hour of the tank's explosion, most of the injured were on their way to hospitals or in the care of local doctors, and many of the dead had been extricated from the morass and removed to the city morgue for identification. Corpses covered in molasses would require significant cleansing before they could be identified, a process that began as soon as the bodies arrived at the morgue. Others were recognized largely by the location in which they were found. Mrs. Bridget Clougherty of 6 Copps Hill Terrace, for example, was found in her home after the building collapsed around her, striking her head, and burying her in debris. Hers was the first building affected by the blast of wind as the tank ripped open, creating a vacuum that yanked her house into the street and wrested it apart. "It fell into a heap of ruins beneath the Elevated structure, where the uprights were broken," the *Globe* noted. "Mrs. Clougherty was picked up and carried across Commercial st and dropped, where the roof of her home fell upon her, crushing out her life." Her husband and two children happened to be out of the house when the wave turned their home into a pile of rubble.

George Layhe, engineer on the Engine 31 fireboat, was inside the firehouse when the molasses hit it and had not emerged when the commander called the roll later that afternoon. His colleagues found him imprisoned under debris in the firehouse wreckage, where he had become trapped when the second floor fell onto the first floor as a solid slab. Despite his efforts to keep his head above the surface of the molasses surrounding him, he finally succumbed even as his crewmates attempted to save him.

"At the Haymarket Relief Station, a great crowd gathered as ambulances, express wagons and drays rushed up with the molasses-coated victims swathed in robes and blankets," the *Globe* reported. "The hospital force was swamped and the conveyances with victims waited in line on Canal st to get into the ambulance entrance at the side of the hospital. . . . About 50 sailors who were passing along the street near the Relief Station and doctors from the U.S.S. *Rockport*, who were near the hospital, hurried into the Relief Station and gave what assistance they could, the bluejackets acting as hospital orderlies. Several army surgeons also gave aid." As often happens in large-scale disaster situations, at least one clergyman, Reverend Father Weiss, S.J., from St. Mary's Catholic Church, rushed to the hospital and made himself available to administer last rites to those who might not live through the day.

In all, 21 people died and more than 150 sustained injuries in what would become known as the Great Molasses Flood—or in some circles, the Boston "Molassacre." The *Globe* totaled the damages in its main edition the day after the disaster: a financial loss of $500,000, including the $225,000 loss of an estimated 1.5 million gallons of molasses (later determined to be 2.3 million gallons), $35,000 damage to the elevated railway structure, six wooden buildings demolished and others "so weakened that they will have to be replaced," and "scores" of city department horses, "which were quietly munching their hay in their stalls, were smothered by the molasses where they stood, while others were crushed and fatally injured by falling timbers."

As quickly as the tank had laid waste to the waterfront district, however, the work to clear the debris and return some kind of normalcy to the area began—and expediency was absolutely necessary, as the molasses had begun to harden with exposure to the cold January air. James B. Shea, chairman of Boston's parks and recreation department, called in contractors to bring dozens of laborers to the scene with heavy-duty trucks, to gather the wreckage of the demolished buildings and vehicles and find whatever could be salvaged. Police officers went through the destroyed residential apartments and offices and retrieved cash, bonds, and insurance policies. They also found and rescued additional people who had been trapped in their homes by the molasses flood, including Tetrina Mercurio and her three children, one of them a baby. Just down the road from the Mercurio family, six young women working in an office of the Bay State Railway leapt from their chairs when every window in the office shattered at the same time; they attempted to leave the building, but molasses poured in the windows and doors and filled the room, trapping them in place. Several of them managed to work their way out through a rear door and climbed a fence to save themselves, but the last one, Elma Van Ward, could not get to the door. Firemen discovered her still in the office, terrified but unhurt.

What was to be done with more than two million gallons of molasses in the streets? Firemen began the seemingly impossible job of spraying powerful streams of water on the gooey liquid, diluting it enough to make it runny and washing it into the sewers and the harbor. As many as 325 workers supplied by the city, the elevated railway company, and the Hugh Nawn Construction company—the corporation that built the tank—labored to remove the remains of buildings and vehicles destroyed in the flood, making it marginally easier for emergency workers to search for additional victims. The body of eighteen-year-old Eric Laird appeared on Friday, January 17, in a morass of ruined boxes and packages in a shed belonging to the Bay State Electric Freight Railway. News reached the *Globe* that Ray Martin, one of the men rushed to a local hospital, had died of his injuries, bringing the death toll to thirteen. Five people remained missing by the newspaper's deadline on Saturday, January 18.

Firemen used salt water from the harbor to wash the molasses out of the streets, staining the harbor brown as the stuff broke down and dissipated. "Ever since the flood of molasses broke loose Wednesday noon and spread over a great area, the workers have been experiencing handicaps and hardships in removing the molasses-covered debris," the *Globe* said on Saturday. "Notwithstanding that firemen constantly played streams from the street hydrants upon the entire neighborhood and upon the heaps of tangled, twisted wreckage, it was not until the city of Boston ordered powerful streams from the fireboat at noon yesterday that the ill-smelling and all-pervading substance began to disappear."

By this time, much of the remaining molasses had hardened, forcing workers to attack it with chisels and ice picks. "Inside the freight houses streams of water were played for hours over the mass . . . upon the broken and wrecked wagons and trucks and upon the carcasses of a dozen horses," the *Globe* said on January 18. "Laborers, equipped with stiff brooms, shovels and hoes, worked unceasingly to remove the covering of molasses." Eugene N. Byington, master mechanic with the Boston fire department, brought two hydraulic syphons to the scene to clear molasses from the cellars of tenement houses on Commercial Street in a search for additional bodies. "The molasses in the cellars is several feet deep and is covered by water," the *Globe* reported. "The water came out quickly, but the molasses is moving very slowly, and it will be hours before the firemen can get in and make a thorough search."

It was this scene of controlled chaos in Boston's North End to which the first officials from USIA arrived on Friday, January 17. Puleo tells us in *Dark Tide* that a contingent led by USIA vice president M. C. Whittaker ended up in a "heated argument" with Thomas F. Sullivan, Boston commissioner of public works, about whether USIA would supply workers to clean up the mess. Whittaker finally agreed, albeit reluctantly, to hire 150 people to assist and remove the pieces of the fragmented tank. Puleo says that Whittaker, stopped by a reporter after the meeting, let his anger dictate his response to the obvious question: How did the accident happen? "If I could [tell you that], I wouldn't have to work for a living," he barked at the reporter.

Days passed before all the bodies of the missing emerged from the wreckage. Ten-year-old Pasquale Iantosca was discovered crushed behind a railroad freight car. Flaminio Gallerani, thirty-seven, finally turned up under water in a Bay State Railroad freight house. Several people who were seriously injured perished in hospitals from infection or pneumonia. The last person whose health was severely compromised in the accident, Stephen Clougherty, died in December 1919 in a mental hospital.

Mayor Andrew J. Peters promised a probe into the tank collapse and delivered one, calling in experts from industry and the military to investigate. Some concluded that the tank must have been the subject of sabotage by anarchists as they pressed their radical agenda, specifying that a ten-pound dynamite bomb detonated from the inside was the only thing that could have resulted in such destruction. With dozens of bystanders at the time of the molasses flood noting that they did not hear any explosion, however, the rest of the scientists and inspectors examining the tank's remains determined that it had undergone a structural collapse. No one had inspected the tank in any official capacity since its installation on December 31, 1915, and while some of the experts noted that the tank had been filled to capacity on a number of occasions and had held up without incident, others agreed that the structural issues must have accumulated over time, with the tank weakening a little more with each capacity load. "Every time the tank was filled with molasses and emptied there was a bending back and forth of the lap joints which in time was bound to weaken the joints beyond the position of safety," wrote auditor Hugh Ogden, who presided over the 1925 court case to determine who was responsible for the accident.

Rubble is all that's left of a fire station on January 16, 1919, the day after a giant tank in the North End collapsed, sending a wave of an estimated 2.3 million gallons of molasses through the streets of Boston. (Courtesy *Boston Globe* via Getty Images)

He concluded, "I believe and find that the high primary stresses, the low factor of safety, and the secondary stresses, in combination, were responsible for the failure of this tank."

USIA paid $628,000 in damages to the 119 plaintiffs in the lawsuit, or roughly $9.5 million in today's dollars. This eased the financial burden on families whose lives were forever changed by the injuries they sustained, as well as on the spouses and children of some of the dead. Many of these people, however, would never recover from the physical and emotional trauma of the most bizarre accident in Boston's history—indeed, one of the strangest and most devastating in the history of any city in the United States.

## CHAPTER ELEVEN

# "Widespread Disaster"— The Great Vermont Flood of 1927

I f you skipped this book's introduction, and you've read diligently to this point, you may believe that the least disaster-prone state in New England is Vermont. It's true that as the only state in the region with no coastline on an ocean or sound, Vermont generally misses the worst of the hurricanes and blizzards, and its largely rural composition allows storms to pass through without causing year-upon-year damage to large communities.

No region on earth gets by without its share of weather events, however. Vermont has experienced its own episodes of destruction in nature's wake—just ask historians in Rutland, Montpelier, and Barre about the torrential rains of November 2 and 3, 1927, when seven to nine inches fell in just eighteen hours after the wettest October in the state's history.

The hurricane season should have been over by the first of November, but the weather had one more major storm to expel before it moved on to winter blizzards. That storm made its way up the Connecticut River valley on November 1, bringing several inches of rain to Connecticut and Rhode Island and to western Massachusetts. When it reached Vermont, however, the tropical storm ran smack into two chilly high pressure systems, one from the east and one from the west. The collision forced the storm into a standstill, leaving it sitting over the ridge of the Green Mountains while it wrung out every drop of moisture it contained.

Montpelier, Vermont's capital city, saw some of the worst damage during the 1927 flood. (Courtesy Library of Congress)

This new rain event quickly topped off water levels that had already risen to new highs a week before, as 150 percent more rain than in a normal October filled every waterway in the state. The heavy downpour began at about 11:30 p.m. on November 2. In and around Rutland, just west of the state's center, swollen streams swelled even more, and by Thursday afternoon, November 3, the first stream flooded. "The rivers quickly overflowed their banks, spread over meadows and farm lands in the first bottoms, and filled many of the valleys from hill to hill," wrote H. B. Kinnison of the US Geological Survey. "The grades of the streams are so steep that excessively high velocities were attained, and the rushing waters washed out bridges, retaining walls, dams, road embankments, buildings, and farm lands. In many sections of the mountainous country near the headwaters the flood peaks arrived suddenly and at night, the inhabitants were taken unawares, and many were unable to reach safety before being drowned in their homes."

Streets became rushing rivers, washing right through automobiles parked along curbs as the waters continued to rise. Soon the flow from East Creek, Moon Brook, and Tenny Brook reached nearby homes in

Rutland, filling basements and first floors, driving residents out of their houses and up onto their roofs.

Firemen launched boats equipped with ladders into the streets, helping people crawl off their rooftops or out through second story windows, and then across the rushing water using the ladder as a bridge. Rain pelted their every step, falling so hard it became difficult to see through it to find stranded residents. "In one place on Granger street where Moon brook crosses, a family of eight children was taken from the second story of a house by stretching the 126 foot aerial ladder across the raging torrents," the *Burlington Free Press* reported the next morning. By late evening on Thursday, November 3, the fire department had completed more than one hundred rescues, and they continued to work through the night to find and save everyone they could in the afflicted area.

Still the water rose. Three miles to the northeast at one of the city's electrical power stations, Glen Dam broke, allowing the engorged stream behind it to pour into Rutland. Railroad lines washed out, forcing the Delaware & Hudson and the Rutland railroads to cease operations. Several miles south in Dorset, railroad companies discovered a massive landslide that covered the state's auto highway as well as the railroad tracks, ending any hope of keeping the trains running. No one could get into or out of the city, and trains already headed for Rutland found themselves stalled at Dorset or marooned to the north, above the burst dam and the floodwaters.

When water flooded the hydroelectric plant, the electrical power supply to the entire city went dead, and employees used every available rowboat to paddle for their lives once they realized they could do no more to keep the plant running. "There will be no electric service for several days and only a limited amount of gas for heating and cooking purposes is available," the Burlington paper said on Friday morning, November 4. "There is no way of pumping the fuel through the mains of the city." Restaurants closed early Thursday evening, finding themselves in the dark and unable to cook even by candlelight. Any accommodation on higher ground became particularly desirable, so hotels and rooming houses filled to capacity, doing their best to provide dry lodging to residents rescued from their homes.

As emergency personnel and newspaper reporters made their way around the city in whatever boats they could press into use, they began to understand the full scope of the damage. Industrial materials from manufacturing plants washed out into the streets as floodwaters rushed through the factories, scooping up all manner of wood, metal, textiles, and machinery and carrying it on the stream's powerful current. Firemen discovered heaps of materials deposited wherever it managed to catch on buildings and cars. "The Howe Scale Company suffered heavily when several thousands of feet of timber were washed down stream and other huge piles in their storage yards were toppled and twisted," the *Free Press* said.

By the Burlington newspaper's press time early Friday morning, Rutland had become isolated, its areas of higher ground literally islands in a rushing stream of rising waters. A bridge collapse on North Main Street and deep water stretching three miles north blocked passage out of Rutland to Burlington. Other bridges on the roads to New York State had washed away as well, while some remained intact but weakened, rendering them useless until they could be inspected more closely. Two bridges on Sherburn Pass on the highway to Woodstock had broken, ending any traffic going east. To the south, where a landslide had already blocked the railroad, bridges on the main road and one farther south over Cold River had failed. Even the road to Bennington had become impassable, its bridges damaged or too precarious to risk. Not only could no one leave the city, but no one could get into the city either, leaving Rutland on its own with no help from emergency responders in neighboring communities until the waters receded.

Where, then, was the Burlington newspaper getting its information? The reporters and pressmen of the *Rutland Herald*, running on a borrowed press with jury-rigged power from a farm tractor, continued to write reports and hand-set type far into the night to make certain that the outside world knew what was happening in its town. "For more than half a century the paper has not missed an issue, even publishing when the plant was completely destroyed by fire," the *Free Press* praised its dedicated comrades.

The *Rutland Herald* itself picked up the story from there, reaching its readers early on the morning of November 4. "This morning, the

View of the Winooski River from the Burlington side from 1927. Seen is the old mill that was a branch of the American Woolen Company (later converted to Forest Hills Factory Outlet) and the pontoon bridge after the November 1927 flood. Building to the left may be the heavily damaged Johnson Grain Co. (University of Vermont Digital Photo Collection)

Herald comes out under flood conditions, partly set from fonts of type furnished by neighborly contemporaries, printed on the press of the Evening News," it said. "Necessarily, the amount of general and local news is limited because, (1) apart from the type set on The Herald's machines before the flood cut off the power, nothing but hand set type was available; (2) because, lacking its battery of six electrically operated typesetting machines, it was physically impossible to get more news into type by the process of setting by hand. A catastrophe like that which has stricken Rutland and its surroundings quickly shows the type of neighbors a newspaper or citizen has, and long before the worst about the flood was known, members of tFe [*sic*] Tuttle company organization had offered the [f]acilities of their plant. Later A. J. Novak gave us the use of his fonts of hand type and half a score of other agencies opened their establishments for necessary supplies."

Thus began a litany of rescue stories, each more heartwarming than the last. The first call for help came from a home near Moon Brook, where eight children and their parents had become trapped by rising waters. Firemen rushed to the scene with a boat and an aerial ladder and managed to retrieve the entire family without a serious mishap. As some families fled their homes in advance of the flood, would-be rescuers waded up to their necks in the roiling water in an attempt to save four men trapped on the roof of their Cleveland Avenue house. The current kept them from reaching the men safely, but someone finally threw a line to the men—none of whom could swim—and towed them off the roof and, apparently, into a boat, which brought them safely to dryer land.

The Knights of Columbus and Elks organizations' lodges had escaped the flooding, and the members lost no time in throwing the buildings open to anyone needing a place to stay. The Howe Scale Company provided its employees and trucks to the fire department to assist in rescue efforts, even as the company began to calculate its own losses of raw materials and merchandise.

One particularly level-headed man appeared in the street as he ran from his inundated home, holding high over his head items he clearly thought would be of greatest value in the current circumstances: a pie in one hand and an assortment of doughnuts and muffins in the other. He didn't bother with extra clothing, keepsakes, or other valuables, the *Herald* noted, perhaps understanding that household goods would only be cumbersome, and most were already too waterlogged to matter. Food, on the other hand, would be at a premium as the city's roads and railways shut down one after another.

As Rutland's mayor Arthur W. Perkins declared martial law and deployed the Vermont National Guard to assist in the rescues and keep people away from the water, the local armory became a mess hall for anyone needing food and a shelter for residents who suddenly found themselves refugees. Captain G. Cecil Ackley commanded the guardsmen, dispatching them to areas still under water to find those left homeless by the flooding and inform them of the availability of shelter and food at the armory. Some also assisted firemen with rescue work, laying ladders from boats to roofs for stranded residents to crawl across.

Refugees, some clutching a few belongings they managed to gather before being forced from their homes, began to straggle into the armory at about 7:00 p.m. Mary A. Devlin, Red Cross nurse, immediately took charge of the young children who arrived alone, distraught, and frightened about where their parents might be, making sure they got dry clothing and caring for whatever injuries they had sustained. She directed everyone, children and adults alike, to the dining room for a hot meal before they were assigned to other rooms with army cots and blankets. "Scores of these emergency beds were filled by 9 o'clock," the *Herald* reported.

By the time the *Herald* went to press with its abbreviated four-page November 4 issue (at about 2:00 a.m. on November 4), officials had already begun to estimate the cost of repairing and replacing their power and transportation systems. An early estimate of $500,000 (roughly $7.1 million in 2021 dollars) covered the power plant, the Manning Manufacturing Company, and the railroads, while private industry and residential losses would come later. (This estimate turned out to be quite below the mark—in all, the state of Vermont suffered damages requiring more than $28 million to repair, and that's in 1927 dollars.)

The *Herald* declared one fact to be beyond dispute, however: this was "the worst flood disaster in the history of the city." One hundred families had been forced to leave their homes overnight to an uncertain fate, with waterlogged walls and belongings just the start of their woes.

Officials predicted it might take days or longer to restore electrical power and to repair some two hundred telephone lines crippled by the flood, a problem compounded by the Glen Dam knocking out the power station at Mill Village and the threat of the Chittenden Dam breaking as well. "Menaced by the rising waters in the Chittenden high in the mountains, 10 miles northeast of town and with a serious prospect that the huge barrier might be swept away, releasing countless thousands of tons of water, many of the inhabitants in the path of the threatening flood sought refuge on the higher levels of the surrounding hills, taking advantage of whatever shelter afforded," the *Herald* said. "While the dam at the Patch plant was threatened, it was still holding at

View of crumbling stone foundation of the old Winooski Bridge, Winooski, Vermont, 1927 flood damage. (University of Vermont Digital Photo Collection)

a late hour last night although that part of the city was entirely isolated from the rest of the town and reports as to the conditions could not be verified."

The *Burlington Free Press* observed that the power loss may have been a blessing in its own way. "The absence of electric current in the tangle of fallen wire which filled many streets minimized the hazard considerably, according to employees of the power company and members of the fire and police departments."

Automobiles did not fare so well. All the cars parked on the city's streets submerged completely as the waters came, rising too swiftly for their owners to start them and drive them away. Residents with garages left their already inundated cars and fled on foot or climbed onto their roofs to wait for help.

"Poultry houses with their feathered occupants, trees, steps, lumber and countless other items of property were swept away by the swollen streams," the *Herald* noted. The paper also included a report about railroad engineer Henry J. LaParle and Samuel J. Langill, a fireman, whose locomotive became submerged at a siding in the town of Proctor. The two men saved themselves by climbing out the window and up to the top of the engine, where they perched in the pouring rain throughout the night. Rescuers spotted them in the cold light of morning and reached the locomotive in a raft, where they found that the two men were in advanced stages of hypothermia. "They were in serious condition from exposure at the Proctor hospital last night," the Rutland paper noted on Saturday morning, November 5.

Tales of dramatic rescues piled up in local news reports. After the Hammond and Gorham bridges in Pittsford, Vermont, washed away— one of them riding the current for nearly a quarter of a mile north—a group of rescuers including Roy and Joseph Churchill came to the aid of Gilbert Rollins and Harold Lowell, when they became trapped on an iron railroad bridge. "The water rose so swiftly that only the head of the man carrying the rope was above the surface when he reached the bridge," the *Herald* said.

Meanwhile, reports began to arrive from other Vermont cities affected by the flooding. Bristol sent word that it had the highest floods in the town's history—five of its bridges were completely gone. "The Lincoln road is under many feet of water and landslides and washouts have made this highway a veritable wreck," the paper said. "The power dams in the village are weakening and forces of men are frantically endeavoring to strengthen the structure. Families along the river have prepared to leave their homes at a moment's notice."

Bennington fared little better, with at least twenty homes in the lowest part of the city flooded up to their second floors. In Woodstock, the Ottauquechee River crested its banks at its highest level "since the freshet of 1869," its newspaper reported.

An Associated Press report detailed the damage at Bellows Falls as "a picture of havoc and suffering." Record-breaking high water had not yet stopped rising on November 4, and "already a paper mill had been torn from its foundations and carried down the stream, and two bridges were gone. Other mills and bridges were in imminent danger. The dam at St. Johnsbury, above Bellows Falls, had gone out, and this meant at 5 o'clock tonight there would be a further six to eight foot rise in the water at Bellows Falls, presumably the peak. The damage already caused was estimated at $1,000,000."

Railroads, telephone, and telegraph communication were all cut off, but one amateur radio operator had managed to get through to another one in Hudson, Massachusetts, who had shared the information with the AP. The message included information about North Walpole, New Hampshire, just over the border from Bellows Falls: "More than 200 families have been driven from their homes. . . . The arch bridge and toll bridge over the Connecticut River were washed away at the abutments and the railroad bridge is covered by six feet of water." Miraculously, no injuries or deaths had taken place, but the railroad tunnel had become partially submerged, with ten feet of water at the entrance causing a significant hazard to nearby hotels and businesses and the International Paper Company. Already the Babbitt-Kelley paper mill had given way and vanished in the flooding.

Barre had become another center of extreme peril and claimed the first two deaths of the statewide event. Ralph Winters and Gerald Breck, both working at a shoe store in town, ran down to the basement of the store to attempt to save at least some of the merchandise there in advance of the flood. As they gathered up boxes of shoes, however, the waters arrived and filled the basement so rapidly that the men could not escape. Still they fought for their lives, but the flood weakened the building's foundation so much that it simply collapsed. A falling wall struck Winters and Breck, knocking them unconscious and perhaps killing them instantly.

Rutland tallied six deaths during the flooding's first night, and the death toll across the state continued to climb as the weekend wore on. A total of nine people perished in the flooding in Barre, and communities as far south as Westfield, Massachusetts, counted fatalities from the event.

Some of the most dramatic damage took place in Montpelier, however. At 2:20 p.m. on Thursday, November 3, the Montpelier Fire Department sounded the flood signal on its fire alarm, the only warning residents of the state capital got to evacuate as fast as they could. Barely a moment later, the Winooski River crested and overflowed, filling the streets with river water and flooding cellars of homes and businesses.

View of a lot of stone rubble with dislodged tracks and exposed sewer pipes. Damage created by the 1927 flood. (University of Vermont Digital Photo Collection)

City officials confirmed just four hours after the crest that this was the worst flooding Montpelier had seen in ten years, and probably longer. The water continued to rise through the evening and into the night.

"So serious did the situation appear in Montpelier that the employees of the State House, the National Life Insurance Company and other business houses were dismissed from work early in the afternoon," the *Burlington Free Press* reported on Friday evening. Schools closed early as well, allowing children to get a head start on reaching their homes before the worst of the flood arrived. The trolley line to Barre, its cars stuffed with passengers, came to a standstill as water washed over the tracks; people commuting by car found that they, too, could not head home because highways had disappeared under floodwaters.

As the water reached ten feet deep, Montpelier mayor E. H. Deavitt telephoned Mayor C. H. Beecher in Burlington and asked to borrow boats to assist in rescue efforts throughout the capital. The water "had invaded the cellars of nearly all the buildings along the street and was even rising above the first floors," the *Free Press* reported. "In the building in which the telephone exchange is located, the water had put the lights out of commission and the exchange was being operated by lanterns, with the possibility that it would soon be out of commission entirely." Mayor Beecher had boats loaded onto a train to rush to Montpelier, but the tracks were under deep water between the two cities, so no train left the station that night. Montpelier was on its own.

Rumors reached newspapers across Vermont that the Berlin Pond Dam, which contained the reservoir of Montpelier's water supply, had burst, and allowed millions of tons of water to rush down into the city, perhaps obliterating it entirely. If this had happened, the papers speculated, the loss of life might be vast and unbearable, and the seat of state government could be crippled for some time. Not until an airplane chartered by a newspaper in Albany, New York, flew into Montpelier with reporters on board did the true story finally come out: the dam had held, though the banks of the Winooski took considerable damage, permitting floods for the record books to inundate the city.

"The casualties were only three, one of which was Lieut.Gov. S. Hollister Jackson," reporter Edmund P. Howe told readers throughout the region. Jackson, fifty-two years old and a highly respected state leader, made the attempt to get home to Barre on a road that had become flooded by a stream. "Although warned not to continue the lieutenant-governor went on and was seen to step out of his car," the report from the *Barre Times* said. "He fell, and then disappeared in the water. Searching parties which included members of the Vermont National Guard hunted fruitlessly Thursday night for him and found his overcoat." Jackson had died within sight of his house.

Not until Sunday, November 7, did the first reports find their way out of Barre, telling of the significant damage the picturesque town had taken. "The rising waters that followed the heavy rains Thursday became dangerous Thursday night when several small buildings were carried away and jammed against railroad bridges where they helped to dam the streams. Suddenly the water backed into what is known as the old channel and swept through the city proper. Many found themselves cut off from escape. Others on safer ground began the rescue work, first with boats. These proved of little avail and ropes finally were used."

The dismal news also contained reports of uncommon heroism, including the story of former Swedish navy sailor Alex Carlson. He spotted seven people stranded on a point near Main Street and did not hesitate to leap into the water and swim to the group, carrying each one individually to safety. "He disappeared, and was believed to have been lost," the *Rutland Herald* retold the story. "Yesterday morning he was found a half mile away on a flat car, suffering seriously from exposure. He is expected to recover." When Carlson vanished below the surface, one Sarafield McNulty took over the rescue work and saved several people before the chilling water and the current's power sapped his strength. He, too, found himself overcome, but others hauled him out of the water and got him safely to a hospital.

Also on Sunday, a reporter and photographer from the *Boston News* flew low enough over Montpelier for two hours to take a dozen photographs, assuaging fears and ending the rumors about the demise of Montpelier. "People can be seen walking about the streets and at places are groups," newspaperman L. K. Applebee Jr., wrote in the *Rutland Herald*. "Automobiles and teams are plentiful and traffic is regular in all sections. Every street and sidewalk in the business section is dry and the only water to be seen in the city is a puddle in the rear of the city hall."

Bit by bit, Vermonters and their neighbors in New Hampshire and Massachusetts cleaned out the mud and debris in their homes, replenished their cupboards, and went back to work as New England Telephone labored to reconnect thousands of phone lines. Government troops and Red Cross workers arrived to assist in the cleanup and to help restore and rebuild railroad lines and roads, and communities raised funds to supply food, clothing, building supplies, and other assistance to people whose homes were lost in the flooding. Eventually, the federal government provided funds for large-scale rebuilding. Vermont moved forward, its residents marveling that by Sunday of the weekend after the flooding, temperatures dropped, and snow began to fall.

While the death toll statewide did not reach the numbers predicted by pundits and rumormongers, the storm and accompanying floods racked up an abundance of staggering statistics: no less than 1,285 bridges were destroyed by rushing waters, nine thousand people had no homes by the time the water receded, and eighty-four people had died in Vermont alone—fifty-five of these in the Winooski River Basin.

"One very remarkable feature was the rapidity with which the rivers rose," the USGS's Kinnison noted. "There was no time for preparation except in the lower Connecticut Valley, and in many places not even time for escape. Tragedy followed upon tragedy in such rapid succession that the people were stunned and helpless for a time, and the losses of life and property were staggering for an area comparatively so small."

## CHAPTER TWELVE

# "Blown Apart"—The 1938 Long Island Express

Wednesday evening brought to an end what is likely to go down as the most calamitous day in Connecticut's history. As nearly as the crippled communications can indicate, no community of any size escaped damage. New Haven is still dark and battered. The heart of New London is in smoking ruins. Along the shore, the combination of an extraordinarily high tide, described by some witnesses as a tidal wave, and a gale of hurricane force has left behind a shambles of broken trees, shattered houses and smashed boats.

—*Hartford Courant*, September 23, 1938

E veryone and no one saw it coming.

The tropical depression formed off the coast of Senegal in West Africa on September 9, 1938, the sixth storm to do so in a fairly average hurricane season, according to a 2016 report from NOAA's Atlantic Hurricane Reanalysis Project (AHRP). Less than a day later, it had become a tropical storm, a rotating system centered on an area of extremely low barometric pressure. The storm tracked west past the Cape Verde Islands and across the Atlantic Ocean, escaping much notice by anyone but naval and commercial ships at sea—the records of which contributed to the AHRP's twenty-first-century reconstruction of hurricane events.

Gathering strength as it approached the southeastern United States, the storm crossed the threshold into hurricane status on September 15—at least that's what NOAA scientists believe, as ships' reports became scarce when the new hurricane reached the middle of the ocean.

By the time it entered the Sargasso Sea on September 16—the region of the Atlantic Ocean off the coast of the southern United States—ships near Puerto Rico recorded the cyclone, and a Brazilian ship, the SS *Alegrete*, noted the low pressure system a day later and recorded winds of as much as 125 miles per hour. The Saffir-Simpson Hurricane Wind Scale did not come into use until 1971, but today's meteorologists tell us that this storm qualified as a Category 3 well before it reached the North American coast.

As the tropical hurricane tracked west past Turks and Caicos and on toward Puerto Rico, it gained force and momentum, reaching Category 5 strength with sustained winds of 160 miles per hour. However, it began to veer northward and away from the coastline, showing every indication that it would return to the sea and dissipate harmlessly over ocean waters.

Meanwhile, well inland on September 18, a cold weather system took shape west of Chicago, Illinois, and drifted north and eastward, bringing high winds and moist cold air into Canada and New England.

On Monday, September 19, as the violent tropical storm obtained a new level of intensity, the US Weather Bureau, the precursor to today's National Weather Service, located the hurricane 650 miles east-southeast of Miami, Florida. Meteorologists Grady Norton and Gordon Dunn issued storm warnings from Key West to Jacksonville, Florida, and watched for the next twenty-four hours until the hurricane turned northeast as it paralleled Daytona Beach, never coming within 350 miles of the Florida shore. Norton and Dunn issued warnings northward up to Atlantic City, New Jersey, and warned all ships around Jacksonville to stay off the waters. By 7:30 a.m. on September 20, as the hurricane reached the waters 140 miles east-northeast of Cape Hattaras, North Carolina, the Jacksonville, Florida, office of the US Weather Service handed off the storm watch to the office in Washington, DC.

Washington issued additional warnings as far north as Eastport, Maine, but with no ships on the water, the meteorologists there had no way to know just how strong a storm they were monitoring. The seasoned veteran meteorologists called the hurricane a "tropical storm" in their advisories, even as young forecaster Charles Pierce, working on his own at the weather bureau with paper and pencil, realized that the

Floodwaters ripped through Ware, Massachusetts, on the heels of the 1938 hurricane. (Courtesy National Oceanic and Atmospheric Administration [NOAA])

storm had already reached a record low barometric pressure and would lay waste to the land in its path: the coasts of Long Island and New England.

Instead of examining the merits of Pierce's calculations, however, chief forecaster Charles Mitchell and his team of more experienced scientists ignored Pierce and downgraded the threat—just as the storm picked up power and maximized the force of its winds. At 11:30 a.m., the Washington office made an even graver error: it issued an advisory that simply mentioned "gale force winds," discounting the storm altogether.

The experienced professionals in Washington did not realize that the hurricane had encountered the cold weather system, which had become a stationary front on the northeastern coast. They also did not take into consideration the power of the passing jet stream, another mass of colder air that encountered the hurricane on its eastern flank. The collision of warm sultry air from the tropics and cold wind from these two northern weather systems changed the cyclone's direction, turning it north and west and boosting its speed to double the pace of a normal hurricane.

The storm had become an extratropical cyclone, the kind of destructive phenomenon New England had not seen since 1635.

Even as the weather bureau issued its 2:00 p.m. warning of "whole gale force winds," a message that told fishing ships to expect winds of about seventy miles per hour, conditions on Long Island had already begun to sour much more violently than that. Barometric pressure bottomed out, high waves of ten to fifteen feet began to beat the southern shoreline, and winds drove all the loose objects it encountered through the coastal air. People enjoying the Hampton beaches on Long Island on the first day of fall gathered up their belongings and made a run for their homes and vehicles as the wind turned sand into clouds that stung.

Sometime between 2:10 and 2:40 p.m. on September 21, the hurricane—now slowed to a still-catastrophic Category 3, with 120-mile-per-hour sustained winds—made landfall over Bellport, New York, on the southern coast of Long Island. It tracked straight northward up the middle of Long Island at the staggering speed of sixty to seventy miles per hour, moving across the peninsula's twenty-three-mile width in less than an hour. In minutes it scrubbed the narrow landmass of its trees, tore thousands of structures from their foundations, and wiped out entire herds of farm livestock. Montauk, at the island's eastern tip, became isolated as the storm surge washed out roads and covered the narrow strip of land between it and the Hamptons.

Twenty thousand miles of telephone and power lines fell in the violent winds, the Long Island Railroad came to a complete standstill as its tracks vanished under water, and half of the island's famous apple crop was lashed off orchard branches and sent sailing through the air. The winds and inflated tide beat fishing ships to matchsticks where they stood, or sank them to the ocean floor, erasing the entire seafood industry from Long Island. Eastern Long Island's shoreline disappeared under the fifteen-foot storm tide, driving the creation of ten new inlets from East Hampton to Fire Island—one of which, Shinnecock Inlet, became a permanent change to the shoreline's geography.

The storm did all of this damage in about fifty minutes. This colossal destruction had already begun when the weather bureau in Washington sent an advisory saying that a storm was seventy-five miles east-southeast of Atlantic City, and that it would likely pass over Long Island

and Connecticut. The advisory still did not call the storm a hurricane or cyclone, but by this time, even a stronger and more accurate warning would have been far too late to save lives and property. Fire Island already saw its boardwalks being ripped from their pilings beneath the feet of people running for shelter, taken completely by surprise by the sudden surge of high waves and the magnitude of the destruction around them.

As suddenly as it had come, however, the hurricane departed, crossing the water between Long Island's north shore and the southern coast of Connecticut and Rhode Island. Still gaining strength and pushing the high tide of the autumnal equinox in its path, it made landfall between Bridgeport and New Haven at about 4:00 p.m., still churning winds of Category 3 strength at 115 to 129 miles per hour.

Only twice before in its history had the southern New England coast experienced a direct hit from a tropical cyclone, and these storms long predated the residents who clustered along the state's popular shoreline. With no advance warning of the oncoming disaster, the storm surge driven by the approaching cyclone created walls of water that batted away cottages and year-round homes along the coast like crumbs on a countertop. Stamford recorded a storm tide of 14.1 feet above normal, while Bridgeport noted a 12.8-foot tide, and New London saw the highest tide in its history before or since: 10.58 feet above normal.

On the Rhode Island coast, a single-lane causeway on a sandbar connected the mainland with the small community of Jamestown. School bus driver Norm Caswell drove through the torrential rain with eight schoolchildren aboard his bus in an effort to bring them home in the storm, but when he reached the causeway, he found it completely submerged and could drive no farther. This, however, did not stop him from trying; he inched forward into the water until the bus stalled about halfway across. Caswell saw that the towering waves sloshing over the causeway would eventually capture the bus and wash it out to sea, so he made the difficult decision to leave the bus and lead the children across the rest of the way. He carried the two smallest children and instructed the other six to form a human chain, holding hands as the waves washed over them again and again . . . until a colossal wave slapped them apart, and its receding force dragged all six into Narragansett Bay. Caswell

A falling chimney destroyed this residence in Rhode Island. (Courtesy NOAA; donated by Susan Medyn)

clung to the remaining two children, but he lost one of them to the waves and emerged from the water with just one of the eight children. The bodies of the other seven washed up on the beach one by one in the days following the storm.

Connecticut residents along the shore had spent the last several days grappling with flooding from the cold front parked over the coastal states, so when the air pressure dropped and the winds picked up in violent gusts, driving high waves and surging tide against their homes and cottages, they had little time and few resources with which to react. East of New Haven, harbors became waterlogged as one hundred-mile-per-hour gusts drove the heavy storm surge into buildings along the shore, dragging many structures into the thrashing surf. Wave after wave washed away summer homes from the tony Connecticut coast, many with the residents still inside. Bay waters pushed their way up the shoreline and into towns and cities.

Hartford's fire department found itself understaffed and overextended as one resident after another called for help between 4:00 p.m. and 8:00 p.m. The emergency crews taking these distress calls found homes with roofs missing, one home missing its veranda, downed old-growth trees making roads impassable, and flooded cellars—so many, in fact, that assistant fire chief William H. Daley told firefighters to deny requests for help in pumping out the underground rooms. "If we tried to help them all we wouldn't have a man left in the department," he said. Even if his men did pump out the water, he continued, the cellars would fill up again in a short time, making the attempt a waste of effort. He put out a warning to residents not to light their furnaces while their cellars were full of water.

Police officers, meanwhile, were busy working to clear streets where fallen trees and walls of destroyed homes trapped people under them, in hopes of getting ambulances through to the injured. Switchboards were jammed with calls to the police, but they determined that they would only respond to calls from people whose lives were truly in danger. Residents who were frantic about property had to wait their turn as one emergent situation after another rose to the top of the call list.

In Hartford, young John O'Connor took the last step of his life as he tried to leave the M&S Transportation Company's garage on

Wethersfield Avenue in the midst of the storm. He had come from his home next door to visit the drivers who were marooned in the garage until the storm subsided, but when he turned to head back home, the hurricane picked the building up from the ground and slammed it into a neighboring open lot, dashing it to a pile of jagged lumber and steel with twenty-one-year-old O'Connor under it. The young man was one of five people in Hartford who did not survive the storm. Twenty-two others were injured, and many people found themselves with no home to return to once the hurricane subsided.

In Stonington, Connecticut, 275 people aboard the *Bostonian* train found themselves trapped on the tracks in the midst of the storm as blowing debris fell and collected in front of the locomotive, blocking the tracks. Unable to proceed or to leave the train cars as the maelstrom railed around them, they watched in horror as entire houses floated by them on the rising waters. Two people decided they could wait no longer and stepped outside, ready to attempt a dash for the nearest shelter—but they found themselves overcome by the cold water, high winds, pelting rain, and the driving current. The two passengers quickly succumbed to the roiling waters. Crew members did their best to keep the rest of the passengers calm until the storm passed and the water receded enough to allow them to clear the tracks in front of them. The remaining passengers arrived at the next station without further incident.

The town of Glastonbury, Connecticut, had already suffered bridge washouts and flooded roads from days of rain before the hurricane hit. When winds ripped through town, buildings toppled as if they were made of cardboard. The First Congregationalist church came apart in the gale and simply fell over, bringing down its iconic spire—the tallest building in town—in the midst of the rubble. Trees came up by their roots and crashed on the roads, blocking access in and out of town and leaving Glastonbury's residents completely isolated from the rest of the state.

"The only means of travel was by walking," the *Hartford Courant* told readers. Trees "crushed the roofs of homes, others smashed cars and still others dragged down utility wires." Men working their way into Glastonbury on foot provided insights about the condition of residential areas: "Hundreds of buildings had been blown apart in all

Little remained of Pawtuxent Cove after the 1938 hurricane. (Courtesy NOAA; donated by Susan Medyn)

sections of the town. . . . They reported many persons missing." Buildings, especially tobacco sheds, literally flew through the air and fell just as suddenly as they had become airborne, crushing whatever house, car, or person had the misfortune to be in their path. Wind that could lift a house had the potential to carry people off with it as well, so police chief Gorge C. Hall told the *Courant* reporter that "he and several fellow officers locked their arms around the bumpers of the police patrol car to save themselves from being carried off by the wind. Many people related that they had been carried hundreds of feet by the wind." By Wednesday night, streets had become "a tangle of twisted trees, utility wires and washouts," so auto owners fought their way through to their cars and flipped on the headlights to help emergency helicopters find their way into town amidst widespread power outages.

In the town of Fenwick, Connecticut, twenty-five-year-old actress Katharine Hepburn, already famous for her many Hollywood roles, intended to spend some quiet time in her family's seaside home considering the next move in a career that had stalled after a series of box office flops. She and her brother Dick, her mother, and others were at Fenwick when the hurricane arrived, driving Katharine off the beach and into the house even as the building rocked precariously in the gale. She and her family made the split-second decision to climb out the dining room window and escape, minutes before the wind and the sea took the house off its foundation as a unit and carried it away on the surf. Katharine, knowing her father would be worried about them, fought the wind and rain and made her way into town to reach the first working telephone she could find. She recalled the experience in her autobiography:

> My God, it was something *devastating*—and unreal—like the beginning of the world—or the end of it—and I slogged and sloshed, crawled through ditches and hung on to keep going somehow—got drenched and bruised and scratched—*completely* bedraggled—finally got to where there was a working phone and called Dad. The minute he heard my voice he said, "How's your mother?"—And I said—I mean shouted—the storm was screaming so—"She's all right. All *right*, Dad! But listen, the house—it's gone—blown away into the sea!" And he said, "I don't suppose you had brains enough to throw a match into it before it went, did you? It's insured against fire, but not against blowing away!—and how are you?"

The Hepburns returned the following day to the last place they had seen their house on the seashore and managed to salvage Katharine's mother's entire silver tea service and eighty-five pieces of silver flatware. She could not find her Oscar statuette for her *Morning Glory* Best Actress win, however, and she later said she'd lost 95 percent of her personal belongings to the storm surge. (The Oscar turned up later and was returned to her.) She and her family built a new house at Fenwick, and it became Katharine's home until her death in 2003.

Providence, Rhode Island, suffered a massive hit when the winds and storm surge drove Narragansett Bay waters into the city, pouring chest-high water down its main streets. Waters rose two to three feet in a matter of minutes, reaching a higher level than its record height during the Great Gale of 1815. As high winds tore the roofs off buildings throughout the city, workers and shoppers ran for whatever cover they could find in the gloom left by an area-wide power outage. People who had found shelter in buildings reached out to those still on the streets or trapped by rising water, pulling them in through windows. "There was no light and little or no telephone communication; the roofs of the State House, the railroad station and several other large buildings were badly damaged," the *Hartford Courant* reported the following day. "Officials estimated between 15,000 and 20,000 workers were stranded in the city, unable to get transportation to their homes. Even fire signals were inoperable." Electrical wires, yanked from their poles by the wind or broken by falling trees, sparked on sidewalks and turned standing water into pools of potential death. Police warned people to stay indoors and wait until the worst of the danger had passed.

The threat of serious injury or worse did not stop people in Providence from taking advantage of the situation, however. The wind propelling debris into windows resulted in smashed glass all over the city, and the easy access to store merchandise and the general confusion tempted people already long compromised by the Great Depression to loot the affected stores and steal thousands of dollars' worth. When honest people saw this behavior, they attempted to call the police, but downed telephone lines made contact impossible. Many of these opportunists got away with their booty. Even more merchandise ended up in the streets when the worst of the storm had passed, making many impoverished (and now likely homeless) citizens consider it fair game.

At about 4:30 p.m., a new crisis emerged: New London, Connecticut, was on fire. The winds and storm surge drove the *Marsala*, a five-masted ship, into a building on New London's shoreline, short-circuiting the building's electrical wiring and setting it ablaze. Fifteen buildings on Bank Street and two on Pequot Avenue caught the wind-whipped flames. Local firemen, wading up to their chests in floodwaters, could do nothing to stop the conflagration from rushing through the middle of the city, consuming a restaurant and a vacant store in addition to a block's worth of commerce. The Niagara Engine Company lost its home, and the Central Coal Company's full bunkers supplied fuel for their own demise. Luckily, the company's office staff managed to escape unharmed—in fact, no one was seriously injured in what the *Courant*

The storm surge shattered trees and tore them apart, like this one in Rhode Island. (Courtesy NOAA; donated by Susan Medyn)

called a "holocaust," though six families had to be relocated to emergency quarters in St. Mary's Roman Catholic Church.

Connecticut governor Wilbur T. Cross called in two hundred National Guardsmen to assist in bringing the fire under control, as well as some eight hundred volunteer firemen from outside the New London area. Together, this corps of responders managed to extinguish the blaze, but a number of businesses were total losses, including two large furniture stores, Humphrey and Cornell wholesale grocery, a pharmaceuticals manufacturer, two coal yards and a lumber dealer, a wholesale paint dealer, and the Easton-Wilson hardware store.

By midnight, amateur radio operator Clinton B. DeSoto of the American Radio Relay League sent word to the *Courant* that "the river at New London was . . . subsiding and that the fire was under control," the paper reported. "The Third Naval District, with headquarters in New York, had sent a relief party to assist in fighting the fire, Mr. DeSoto said."

Still moving at a high speed, the storm passed over Connecticut and Rhode Island and into Massachusetts, making its way into Vermont by 6:00 p.m. as what the weather service accurately called an "extratropical storm." This somewhat softened system still proved to be the last boost that rivers and streams all over southern New England needed to crest their banks. Swollen from a wet summer and four days of additional rain that predated the hurricane, rivers washed out bridges and roads across inland Connecticut and western Massachusetts. Middletown and Portland, Connecticut, stood helpless as the Connecticut River crested and overflowed into the cities. Factories in Gardner, Chicopee, Athol, and Southbridge, Massachusetts, shut down abruptly as river water rushed onto their manufacturing floors, idling thousands of workers. Schools closed across the region to allow children to stay home until they could be made safe again. Indeed, the incidents outdoors underscored the need for caution: in Gardner, seven people—including an eighteen-month-old toddler—dropped into rushing floodwaters when a reservoir dam burst and the road they were on collapsed. All of them escaped with the help of others in the area, who found themselves pressed into service as first responders. In Southbridge, Massachusetts, as the Quinebaug River crested its banks, rescuers removed more than one hundred people from their homes in boats and motored or paddled them to safety. Farther north, the city of Peterborough, New Hampshire, saw several buildings go down in flames as wiring short-circuited by floodwaters set off the wooden structures.

Soapstone, Massachusetts, saw an even more dramatic accident caused by the flooding. Waterlogged and weakened, a hillside east of the Hoosac Tunnel gave way and became a formidable landslide. The force of the falling dirt and rocks pushed a twenty-two-car freight train off the tracks and into the Deerfield River. The locomotive and three cars had passed the hillside seconds before it let go, so they missed the sight of an entire wall of soil, rock, and vegetation crumbling at once and rushing through the air toward their windows. The affected cars carried no passengers, so no one was hurt when most of the train slid into the water.

The storm's ability to destroy people and property provided the most dramatic early reports of hurricane damage, but not until the storm passed out of New England did its magnitude there become clear. Entire forests were leveled, devastating fruit crops and denuding much of the landscape. Some neighborhoods emerged unscathed, but others appeared completely wiped out, pieces of their homes strewn over the landscape and single walls or chimneys left standing alone. Communication systems had been scraped off the state's surface, tangled into knots with timbers and boards from deconstructed buildings and left clustered in the middle of roads. Receding flood waters revealed even more destruction, leaving piles of mud, rocks, sand, tree branches, and the debris of ruined houses in yards, gardens, and basements, and shoved through smashed windows of homes.

Government officials moved quickly to unleash thousands of workers to begin cleanup, repair work, and rebuilding of fortifications against future floods, and to care for thousands of people left homeless by the hurricane. Communities like Norwich, Connecticut, one of the hardest hit, found themselves with waterlogged markets and warehouses full of food rendered inedible by floodwaters. "On short rations, under military patrol and curfew, living in fear of typhoid and hunting out profiteers, Norwich Friday started fighting its battle to recover from the $2,000,000 wallop it got from hurricane and tide Wednesday," the

The tug *Monhegan* rode into the middle of Providence's streets on the storm surge. (Courtesy NOAA; donated by Susan Medyn)

Woods Hole, Massachusetts, took a serious beating from the hurricane's violent storm surge. (Courtesy NOAA)

*Hartford Courant* reported on September 24. "Its wholesale provision houses flooded 11 feet deep and contents destroyed, the town is short of food and will remain so for days. Restaurants are allowed four loaves of bread and four dozen buns a day. . . . If you want to buy provisions in the stores that remain open you must live in the nearby area and they will let you have just one day's supply. Profiteering will be promptly punished." Nurses and doctors from throughout the region rushed to the stricken areas to provide vaccines against typhoid, setting up emergency immunization bureaus to reach as many people as possible and instructing residents to boil water in their homes before using it.

Fraternal organizations and armories opened their doors to accommodate people whose homes were destroyed, staffing them with volunteers and workers from the federal government's Works Progress Administration (WPA). The WPA's female employees cooked meals, made and distributed clothing and blankets, and provided cots and other small comforts until people could make some kind of living arrangements.

The WPA had spent time in southern New England just two years earlier, when widespread flooding from a particularly wet spring and summer had devastated communities. They had built dams and other fortifications against river flooding, but these structures were no match for the swollen tide and powerful storm surge the hurricane supplied. The WPA returned to some of the same areas after the hurricane, as well as to the coastal cities and towns hardest hit by the storm. "Two WPA shifts work night and day to remove flood debris, brick piles from structures knocked down on several streets, and muck and trees," the report from Norwich said, just one of the many areas in which thousands of workers toiled to clear roads and began to restore order. They discovered mangled automobiles, roofs, and downed trees as they dug through the sand, mud, and rock the tide had shoved in its own path, making every inch of cleared road a hard-won battle. It would take two years for workers to clear the last of the hurricane debris from Connecticut and Rhode Island shores.

Hardly a day passed after the storm before New England residents and the media began looking for someone to blame.

An unnamed editor of the *Hartford Courant* wrote a gripping editorial on September 23, pointing its finger at US representative Herman P. Kopplemann for sinking a flood control bill in Congress after widespread flooding in 1936 had devastated many areas of Connecticut. "The regional flood control compact, which would have given Hartford a measure of protection by holding back the excess water that poured into the river from the saturated ground, was killed, and Representative Kopplemann has boasted that he was in large part responsible for its demise," the editorial said. "The Hartford Flood Control Commission has prepared a comprehensive program of dikes, which would not only protect the city against floods ten feet higher than the present flood is likely to go, but would have reclaimed about a fifth of the city that is now not available for new construction because of the threat of high water."

More widespread, however, was the call to determine why the US Weather Bureau had not warned the people of Long Island and New England that such a powerful storm was on its way, even when it had already begun to pound the coast. The Weather Bureau attempted a defense that pointed fingers back at New Englanders, saying that more advance warning would not have helped them because they were not "hurricane-minded"—implying that the people of Connecticut and

Rhode Island would not even have known how to take the proper precautions. No one at the Washington bureau lost their job over the shocking error of ignoring young Charlie Pierce's calculations, but chief forecaster Charles Mitchell did retire shortly after the incident, and Pierce, the only one who had seen the hurricane coming, moved up in the ranks.

As communities across the region tallied the damages, the cumulative statistics outpaced any other disaster New England had ever faced. The storm itself became the standard against which all other hurricanes would be measured: maximum sustained winds of 121 miles per hour, with a wild 186-mile-per-hour gust at the Blue Hill Observatory in Massachusetts (measured just before the wind speed device broke off); a low pressure reading of 27.94 inches (946.2 millibars) in Bellport, New York, the lowest ever recorded in that area. Rhode Island saw the peak storm surge at seventeen feet above a normal high tide, and the highest waves arrived at Gloucester, Massachusetts, where they crested at fifty feet.

Even more impressive and debilitating were the losses of life and property. Nearly 700 people died in the storm, most of them by drowning, and as many as 1,800 suffered serious injury. Nearly 19,000 buildings and homes were destroyed on Long Island and in New England, leaving 63,000 people homeless. Thirty-three hundred vessels were lost at sea, as many as 26,000 automobiles were crushed or rendered unusable, and more than 275 million trees fell in the driving winds— enough to creating 2.6 billion board feet of useful lumber, which quickly became a tool in the region's reconstruction. The falling trees took down some 20,000 miles of electrical and telephone lines, cutting power to nearly every home and business in the region and knocking out telephone service to one-third of New England.

"Across New England, mature parkland elms and conifers fell at college campuses such as Wesleyan University in Middletown, Connecticut; Dartmouth College in Hanover, New Hampshire; and Worcester Polytechnic Institute in Worcester, Massachusetts," a retrospective report by Risk Management Solutions (RMS) said. "The town common of Amherst, Massachusetts, which is home to Amherst College, lost 3,000 trees." Iconic landscapes that attracted students and tourists had been stripped of their majesty, a loss that would take decades to restore.

Members of the WPA workforce look through the wreckage of homes for bodies. (Courtesy NOAA; photo by Steve Nicklas)

The damages amounted to more than $7 billion in 2021 dollars, and some areas would never recover—Napatree Point, Rhode Island, once a picturesque village of summer cottages, became a wildlife preserve after the storm wiped it clean of all of its buildings. Napatree's slender, 1.5-mile sand spit in Block Island Sound ended at Sandy Point before the hurricane, but the storm surge turned Sandy Point into an island in Little Narragansett Bay. Watch Hill, the village near Napatree, virtually disappeared in the storm surge, while massive waves freed clusters of homes from their foundations along the coast in Westbrook, Old Saybrook, and Old Lyme, Connecticut, carrying them out to sea. Warehouses, docks, and piers along the Connecticut, Rhode Island, and Massachusetts coasts saw their underpinnings washed away, leaving them literally without a leg to stand on. On Block Island off the coast of Rhode Island, the fishing fleet lost 70 percent of its boats.

How would New England recover? The one benefit of the Great Depression, it seemed, was the enormous number of willing and able laborers who could be recruited immediately to put the region back together. Tens of thousands of workers, supervised by the WPA, the Civilian Conservation Corps, several branches of the military, the National Guard, and private enterprise set to work clearing and burning debris, shoveling mud and sand off roads and onto trucks to be returned to the coastline, transporting fallen trees to working sawmills, and beginning the process of rebuilding. A woeful 5 percent of homeowners and businesses had insured their property, so many factories never reopened, changing the nature of business and employment in Connecticut, Rhode Island, and Massachusetts for thousands of workers. Some families packed up and moved away, never to rebuild the homes they lost. Others repaired the damage and moved back into their homes, noted the *Hartford Courant* on October 5, 1938, just two weeks after the storm had evicted so many inhabitants. Three-quarters of the damaged homes in Hartford had been made habitable again, and the Hartford Health Department had reopened for occupancy 502 of the 530 buildings made unsafe by the storm and floods.

Rhode Island officials worked closely with the WPA and other federal agencies to make its way back from the flooding. The Northern Rhode Island Farm Bureau made a deal with a government agency to sell it fifty thousand bushels of apples blown out of trees during the storm at seventy-five cents a bushel, a literal windfall for orchard growers. City councils throughout Rhode Island struggled to find the money they needed to rebuild infrastructure, canceling projects like an addition to a high school in Newport to redirect funds to storm rehabilitation. By October 1, Rhode Island had filed applications to the Public Works Administration in Washington for grants totaling more than $30 million for "schools, hospitals, waterworks, bridges, sewers, and the like," the *Newport Mercury* reported on October 7. This sum represented just half of what the state needed to replace its damaged or entirely obliterated systems.

Months passed before southern New England returned to something like the normalcy it had enjoyed before the hurricane. To this day, however, the Long Island Express remains the most devastating storm in New England history, one that has not yet seen its match—but that may be challenged in the future as climate change ramps up more volatile, frequent, and widespread storms.

"No matter the uncertainty in the size and timing of a major hurricane making landfall along the coastline of the northeastern U.S., it will happen again," the evaluation by RMS concluded. "It is imperative to educate the communities on the potential impacts and prepare well in advance of an impending storm. . . . A major hurricane will strike New England again; only uncertainty in the size and timing of the event remains."

## CHAPTER THIRTEEN

# "End of the World"— The Week Maine Burned in 1947

It's impossible to talk about traumatic events in New England without addressing the great fire of 1947, the one that burned two hundred thousand acres of Maine's forests and transformed towns including Bar Harbor and most of York County in a weeklong rampage of wind, heat, and flame.

What must happen to create such a fire? Reports cite major blowdowns of dead tree limbs, leaves, and entire trees knocked over by hurricanes as far back as 1938, left to dry and accumulate throughout the densely forested state. Couple this with a summer-long drought that extended into mid-fall, during which state officials ordered fire watch towers to remain open a month beyond their usual September closing as one hot, sunny day followed another in a totally uncharacteristic New England autumn.

At first, the cloudless summer seemed like a wonderful gift after a particularly rainy April, May, and June. The last significant rain of the summer fell in mid-July 1947, and nearly three months of balmy, sunny days followed one after another, marked by "one of the most glorious Indian summers in living memory," said Joyce Butler in her book *Wildfire Loose: The Week Maine Burned.* The usual fall rains did not materialize, even as September ended and the shorter days and colder nights of October arrived. October, in fact, remained unseasonably warm with less than one-tenth of an inch of rain, and leaves changed color, fell to the ground earlier than normal, and crumbled into dry powder almost on contact.

Maine residents knew well that such an arid summer and fall could lead to forest fires, but on Mount Desert Island, long an idyllic escape for wealthy summer folk who owned mansions in Bar Harbor and in the island's other towns, most of the summer people had already packed up to return to New York City, Boston, and other major commerce centers. They were largely unaware of the climate in Maine once they were gone and made no plans to protect their vacation homes in the event of a fire, a hazard that had never been a serious consideration in Maine's verdant forests.

Year-round residents, however, saw all kinds of perils in the dust rising from schoolyards and the arid soil in farmers' fields. Ponds and streams stood at historic low levels, wells had begun to go completely dry, and state and local parks placed bans on campfires and smoking in the woods. Dairy farmers struggled to keep their livestock watered. "They bought every empty vinegar and molasses barrel the local stores had to sell and made two or three trips a day to the nearest water supply," wrote Butler. One farm in Norway, Maine, faced a dry well for the first time in history, leaving no water for 1,800 turkeys and 20 cattle.

In Acadia National Park at the heart of Mount Desert Island, the National Park Service had hosted a firefighting school right in the park in May, bringing firefighters from Yellowstone National Park—a park with a high incidence of massive forest fires—to train the Bar Harbor Fire Department and park service employees in the most up-to-date techniques for fire control. Bar Harbor's firefighters had the opportunity in August to use what they'd learned, quickly extinguishing fires in the town of Hulls Cove. All the firefighting professionals in the area felt confident that they could face the usual brush fires and other localized flare-ups as they happened, even in an autumn as dry as this one.

As the dry season extended into October, the first small fires sparked into life on October 7 in brushy woods in Wells, Bowdoin, and Portland, all in southern Maine's York County. With thirty miles and more between these three cities, firefighters immediately recognized that vast areas of the state could be in danger of catching fire separately and simultaneously, causing the kind of widespread emergency that would tie up every resource they had to keep blazes under control. Their worst fears began to come to pass in the next few days as fire tower observers, farmers, and townspeople began to report small fires throughout the county and beyond—and by the middle of the month, forest fires had begun to rage throughout the southern and eastern counties of the state.

No sooner was one fire brought under control than another one flared up somewhere else. The *Biddeford Daily Journal* carried an Associated Press (AP) story on October 15 warning that "Tinder-dry woods became a serious fire hazard in widely separated sections of New England today," listing forest fires burning in Massachusetts, Maine, and New Hampshire. "Vermont's governor Ernest W. Gibson suspended the hunting season because of the hazard—the first such action in that state since September 1941," the newspaper said. "Fires burned last night in Fairhaven, West Boylston, Holliston and Byfield [Massachusetts]. . . . Ten fires burned in Maine, the largest over a 100-acre area in the Topsham-Lisbon section. . . . State Forest Supervisor Austin Wilkes [*sic*; actually Wilkins] reported fires at Hartford, South China, East Stoneham, Livermore and Appleton." States warned hunters to monitor their own cigarettes and matches carefully, as a thoughtlessly flicked ash could ignite a flame that would spread far and wide before firefighters could reach it.

Professionals and volunteers battled the blazes as best they could, but the fires in Maine took a particularly insidious route: with their flames extinguished in plain sight, they followed tree roots downward and continued to burn underground. Wilkins told the *Portland Press Herald* that "in some places, where water was not accessible, trenching was the only method of fighting the advance of the flames." Firefighters worked to create firebreaks by digging trenches with bulldozers, but the dry earth ran back into the trenches like sand. Fires in Pine Grove, a housing development in Lisbon Falls, "raced to within 500 feet of 30 houses on the east side of the main road before it was stopped." Nearby, a fire already burning for four or five days became larger on October 14, and "ravaged more than 100 acres of small growth and slash. Bowdoin College students were among the volunteers fighting this fire." Falling leaves, normally dampened by autumn rains, dropped brown and crisp to the ground and intensified the hazard, Wilkins told the press, calling them "a menace the instant they strike the ground."

Wind-whipped flames destroy several summer homes at Cape Porpoise, Maine, as a forest fire in the Kennebunkport area raged unchecked, October 22, 1947. More than two hundred homes were destroyed in a five-mile stretch of coastline. (AP Photo)

The first reports of major losses came in on October 15: a farm at South Rumford found itself directly in the path of a fire. The blaze "caused a loss estimated at $20,000," or more than $230,000 today, as it "destroyed a set of buildings owned and occupied by three brothers, Sabin, Carl, and Philip Milligan, with all their contents, 15 head of livestock and 500 chickens and turkeys perishing." The fire rushed through their property in the early morning hours, catching all twelve members of the three families in slumber. "The Milligans escaped in their night clothing," the *Portland Press Herald* reassured its readers. Down the road in Rumford, the AP reported a fire near a boiler at Arthur Breau's dairy milk processing building, causing $8,000 in damage, or the equivalent of $92,000 in modern funds.

Maine's governor told the media on October 15 that he did not see a reason to close the forests to hunting, but the state's forest commissioner saw things differently. Raymond E. Rendall informed the

AP that he was considering a ban on smoking and building fires in the woods, and that he would confer with Governor Horace Hildreth the following evening to determine if the ban would be enough, or if they should close the forests to hunting altogether until a soaking rain made humans in the woods less hazardous. "I have just received reports from eastern, central and southern areas tonight which are disturbing because of the very dry conditions existing in our forests," Rendall said. "It appears that we probably have to do something right away to try to check further outbreaks of fires." That day, New Hampshire joined Vermont in closing its forests to hunting, and newspapers reported that the number of fires burning in Maine alone had reached twenty blazes.

In Centerville, in the heart of paper company holdings in Washington County, Maine, fire burned thirty-three cords of pulp wood before lumber mills began closing to allow their employees to combat the blaze. Fifty firefighters of the Maine Forestry Service fought the flames along the Machias River as the fire sank below ground, traveling along tree roots to pop up suddenly in new areas and kindle new fires above the surface.

Reports from Rockport revealed how difficult it was to fight fires the men could not see. A fire blazing on the west side of Route 1 near the homes of several selectmen and their families seemed to be under control by the end of Wednesday, October 15, but it "broke out anew in the evening traveling underground to the Wildwood Park area on Route One," the Portland paper reported. "City water was being pumped almost a mile through the woods by the Rockport Department. An unestimated [*sic*] area of woodland had been burned over at press time Wednesday night and a strong breeze was hampering efforts of firemen to subdue the blaze."

Reports like these came in from all over the state. A blaze at the base of Blackstrap Mountain quickly burrowed underground and threatened the entire forest there, while several other fires flared up all around Falmouth. Every firefighter in the region and hundreds of volunteers gathered to squelch the flames, but no sooner did they manage to bring one fire under control than calls would come in from other areas about new ones. Some took only a few hours and many thousands of feet of hose to extinguish, while others burned out of control for days. Fire marshals lost no time in reporting to the state forestry office any fires that looked to be set off by carelessness with campfires, cigarettes, and matches.

On Thursday, October 16, Hildreth suspended the hunting season in Maine and "prohibited the building of outdoor fires, except at public campsites maintained by the State Forestry Department." The proclamation canceled the last two days of the duck hunting season and postponed opening of deer hunting the following week. Massachusetts followed suit the same day, and Governor Thomas E. Dewey of New York shut down hunting in the drought-stricken Adirondack Mountains as well, the AP reported.

"The hunting ban was justified in every way," columnist Gene L. Letourneau with the *Portland Sunday Telegram* reassured readers on October 18 in his "Sportsmen Say" column. "Duff in the woods is dust dry, or has been, and the fire hazard more than apparent. Several fires have broken out, destroying with them a number of covers. Loss of these areas by fire means less hunting areas, less game. . . . Because of the record breaking heat, there were no migration of waterfowl during the first season, but conditions should have satisfied northern Maine nimrods who feared that the birds would be frozen out as the result of the Oct. 7 opening date."

Rendall took further action, notifying all the mills in the area that their equipment had to have the proper screens at the tops of their smokestacks to "prevent sparks from flying dangerously into the tinder-dry woods and leaves on the ground." He added, "Conditions are in a high state of inflammability and general throughout the state."

"I particularly urge the cooperation of all woods operators and their crews," Hildreth added in his proclamation. "Upon these people rests a great responsibility to exercise every possible vigilance to guard against fires during this serious situation."

By the following day, however, the news became even bleaker for Maine. No less than sixty forest fires burned across the state, AP reported, and families who lived near the affected woodlands loaded their household goods and valuables into trucks and fled. In Bowdoin, two hundred volunteers managed to bring "a fierce blaze that swept 1,000 acres of timber and slash near route 125" under control before it destroyed farms and property. "A firebreak, chewed by bulldozers out of territory along Larrabee Road, and backfires saved a dozen other houses from the blaze that swept into Bowdoin Center," the final stop for a fire that began on a six hundred-acre tract at Topsham. Fast work by bulldozers across the region kept fires from reaching homes, while veteran fire warden Ivory J. Bradbury, who had retired on October 1, returned to his post to help with twenty-one fires burning across York County alone.

Reports throughout New England painted a terrifying picture. A "spectacular" fire, according to the AP, had crested the top of Mount Tom in Holyoke, Massachusetts, overnight as it burned the "powder dry" forest. Vermont, New Hampshire, and even Connecticut and Rhode Island reported blazes as well. States began to tap into their emergency water supplies to quell the flames and to provide drinking water to towns and cities. Worse, the National Weather Bureau predicted that temperatures would continue to rise into the mid-eighties with no rain in sight. In Boston, the thermometer reached a record-breaking eighty-nine degrees on October 17.

By October 20, the *Portland Press Herald* reported that the fires had finally come under firefighters' control. "Flames had charred more than 25 square miles of woodland in the Brunswick-Topsham area," the newspaper said. "Desperately needing rain to extinguish the stubborn fire, firefighters dynamited a beaver dam in an attempt to increase their dwindling water supplies." At the same time, the Reverend Paul J. West, pastor of West Falmouth Baptist Church, called for a prayer meeting that evening to pray for rain. "Miracles are possible if people are in earnest," he said, hoping to defy weather forecasts that still saw no clouds ahead.

Wilkins told the media on October 20 that the Shapleigh-Waterboro fire appeared to be contained as well, "where roughly 2,500 acres of pitch pine and scrub oak were burned over with no serious loss. The fire was surrounded after 10 tank trucks and three bulldozers, the latter digging ditches, had been used."

James F. King, a journalist with the AP's Boston bureau, flew in a plane chartered by the news organization over the burning landscape on October 22. "A 50-square-mile area of southeastern Maine looks today like a petrified forest," he wrote. "Huge clouds of billowing smoke, so dense that our pilot has had to fly on instruments part of the way, are blowing out to sea in the early morning northwest wind, revealing the extent of the damage from yesterday's roaring forest fire which raged unchecked to the shoreline, wiping out the summer colony at Goose Rocks Beach."

The fire blazed so hot and so long, King noted, because the drought had made water virtually unavailable to firefighters. He and his pilot spotted no new fires from the air, but veteran forest fire fighters told him that wood fires often looked weaker first thing in the morning, and then grew larger during the day as morning sun dried out the forest. "Then, too, the wind was rising, and threatened to fan into new life the slowly burning remnants of last night's roaring blaze," he said.

The first battles against the flames had been fought and won, but another, even more devastating fight remained on the near horizon. By the following morning, a new headline in the *Biddeford Daily Journal* shocked Maine residents barely beginning to breathe more easily after the initial crisis: "Twenty-Five Homes Burned; Goose Rocks Afire."

By the time the paper went to press, its headline was already out of date: at least one hundred homes along Goose Rocks Beach in Kennebunkport were on fire or already destroyed and three hundred more stood in the path of the new inferno. What had begun as another forest fire joined with a new factor that had not yet plagued the beleaguered state: wind. "Strong winds are fanning the blaze from north to south, and residents of the area, estimated at about 25 families, began mass evacuation, piling furniture and other belongings onto trucks and other vehicles."

Beyond this line of homes and cottages, Cape Porpoise lay in the fire's path, a resort area with many more summer homes. "Firemen have given up hope of controlling the blaze, and are retreating as the fire advances, since the heat of the flames is so intense, they are unable to remain close to them," the report dismally concluded. With the available water already depleted by more than a week of constant firefighting, the firemen and volunteers had little to work with as they faced the fiercest and most destructive conflagration yet.

On Goose Rocks Beach, Mrs. Herbert Emery managed to escape her home before it began to burn and sought refuge down the road in the home of Mrs. John Henchey. The two women were discovered standing knee-deep in the Atlantic Ocean sometime later, as both the Emery home and the Henchey home became engulfed in flames and burned to the ground. Rescuers took the two women to the American Red Cross emergency shelter set up in St. Joseph Hall. Down the road, Mr. and Mrs. John Medina worked frantically to move their furniture from their home, which was surrounded by woods, into an empty cottage nearby. To their dismay, the fire arrived and lit the cottage, turning it and all their furniture to ashes. Their home, miraculously, escaped the flames and emerged without significant damage.

Reports from all over the state grew more frequent and harrowing as the fires became widespread. In Kennebunkport, nearly two hundred buildings had been lost by October 23, including many vacation cottages—and the flames continued to consume the town when Wilkins reported this to the AP.

"Forest fires, the worst of which razed the coastline from Goose Beach to Kennebunkport, have blackened 10,000 acres of valuable timber, scrub growth and slash in Maine's parched forests, a conservative estimate given by a forestry official said today," the *Biddeford Daily Journal* reported as part of its extensive fire coverage on October 22. Later in the same column, the paper noted, "Ladies of the Dame de la Victoire society will assemble at either St. Josephs or St. Andres church this evening at 6:30 to pray for rain."

Overnight, runaway fires destroyed 175 cottages in Kennebunkport at Goose Rocks, Cape Porpoise, and Wildes District, leaving "scores of homeless families," the newspaper reported. No sooner had the flames either found nothing else to consume or succumbed to the efforts of firefighters, however, than looters moved in, taking advantage of the area's desertion to steal "motors from boats, farm equipment and plumbing from cellars of razed Goose Rocks homes," the *Journal* reported. Municipal court judge Kenneth Spencer, a Kennebunkport resident, made a call to Governor Hildreth and asked him to declare martial law, but the governor declined to do so, saying that it seemed the authorities on the scene had the situation in hand. Nonetheless, National Guardsmen took positions throughout the area and turned away anyone who was not a resident or a firefighter.

Volunteers streamed to the front lines to help in any way they could. "Among volunteers battling the blaze are 125 students from St. Louis High school, which dismissed classes this morning, students from St. Frances College, Pool road, and 20 students from the University of New Hampshire," reports said. "Volunteers from the shops and mills in this area as well as members of local civic and fraternal organizations are also working to combat the fire."

Smoke clogging Route 1 and all other roads in areas near the fire became so much of a hazard that police closed the road as a safety precaution. Sadly, this measure did not take place in time to protect thirty-six-year-old Aurele J. Tremblay, a blacksmith in Kennebunk, who was struck by a car driven through the smoke by Raymond Carter of Bangor, and perished in a hospital sometime later.

Three newsreel cameramen narrowly escaped death as they recorded the fire for Paramount and other news organizations, the *Journal* noted. They had taken refuge in one of the homes in the path of the flames as they filmed the fire and had far too close a view of a tree that suddenly exploded, sending flames up some 150 feet into the air. Phil Coolidge, Larry Ellis, and Arthur Gaskell ran for their lives, heading for their car, but when they reached the spot where they had parked it, they found it had vanished. They had little time to chide themselves for leaving the keys in it before they had to run from flames that had jumped the road behind them.

"It was later learned that a newspaperman, Don MacPhail of the *Boston Evening American*, had seen the automobile in danger of catching fire, and had driven it further down the road to make his own escape," the *Journal* discovered.

As Goose Rocks Beach and Cape Porpoise faced the darkest days in their communities' history, another iconic Maine town faced its own crisis, one that would change its complexion for decades to come.

On Mount Desert Island, the first sign of fire revealed itself as a wisp of smoke on October 17, when a woman identified in the records only as Mrs. Gilbert—a resident living about seven miles from Bar Harbor—called the fire department to report smoke rising from the Fresh Meadow cranberry bog between her home and nearby Dolliver's Dump. Fire chief David Sleeper responded immediately, dispatching a

Publisher Joseph Pulitzer, right, with his pilot, unidentified, views the remains of the estate of Mrs. William S. Moore, his sister, at Bar Harbor, Maine, October 24, 1947, after the home "Woodlands" was leveled in the disastrous fire on October 23. (AP Photo/Abe Fox)

150-gallon tank truck to the bog in hopes of dispensing with the blaze quickly. When the driver reached the bog, however, he found the fire had already burned more than an acre of land, Emptying his truck's water on the blaze did not extinguish it. He called the firehouse for backup, and Chief Sleeper sent everyone available to the fire, meanwhile ordering a general alarm. Acadia's park firefighters got the call and sent a fire truck and crew as well.

Together, the Bar Harbor Fire Department and park service personnel got the fire under control, and Bar Harbor firefighters monitored it through the weekend. The cranberry bog fire burned just 169 acres over the course of three days, but it continued to burn underground tree roots, a phenomenon the fire department had no way to control. On Tuesday morning, October 21, however, a new blaze sprang up about two hundred feet away, and a strong northwest wind fanned the flames until they were "spreading with terrifying speed before the wind through a thick growth of spruce and pine," Butler wrote in *Wildfire Loose*. Chief Sleeper put out a call for assistance to every fire department on the island, as well as to Dow Field, headquarters of the US Army's 14th Fighter Wing. A short time later, two hundred men and equipment left Dow Field and headed for Mount Desert Island.

The additional firefighters arrived too late to contain the blaze, however. "At the scene the firemen could not lay hose fast enough to head off the flames that spread rapidly through the spruce and pine trees, crowning forty to fifty feet in the air," Butler wrote. "By the time reinforcements arrived, the fire was completely out of hand."

Forces came together at Eagle Lake Road (Route 233) in hopes of making a strong stand against the fast-moving flames, with access to plenty of water from the lake to keep their supplies up until they could get it under control. At 4:00 p.m., however, the fire leapt past them across the road and began to burn in Acadia National Park's forest. An hour later the flames stretched for three miles along Eagle Lake Road, threatening buildings in the park, including the iconic historic Jordan Pond House, if the winds blew the fire southward.

More professionals and volunteers arrived to battle the blaze, including the US Coast Guard, students and instructors in the University of Maine forestry program, and men from the Bangor Theological Seminary.

Darkness came, blacker than usual because the fire had reached the power transformer that served Mount Desert Island, shutting off the island's electricity. No one in Bar Harbor or the neighboring towns slept peacefully that night. They packed clothing and their most treasured belongings as they waited for warning that it was time to evacuate.

Remarkably, the weekly *Bar Harbor Times* published on schedule on Thursday morning, October 23. "What is the most spectacular forest fire, and possibly the most dangerous that Mount Desert Island has every experienced, threatened the Village of Bar Harbor Tuesday night after traveling from across the highway between Beaver Dam, so-called, and Dolliver's Dump through to the Eagle Lake Road, jumping the Break Neck Drive and straddling the Norway Drive and then turning west with the wind, burned to the edge of Eagle Lake on the south and the new Eagle Lake Road to the east, where the Bar Harbor Fire

Department, assisted by volunteers and apparatus from neighboring towns as far away as Bangor and Brewer, checked it at dawn, Wednesday morning and temporarily ended its threat to advance in the westerly portion of the village proper," the paper's breathless report read.

In the park, Acadia raised the alarm with the National Park Service, which flew thirty-eight wilderness firefighters from New York, Florida, Virginia, Georgia, and Kentucky to Maine to assist in protecting the park, and placed experts from the western parks on standby. Acadia management, the expert firefighters, and Chief Sleeper met on Wednesday afternoon, October 22, and decided that the park service would take control of any firefighting done within the park's borders, relieving the Bar Harbor chief of that responsibility. This allowed him to focus his resources—now swollen to fourteen fire departments from every village on the island—on populated areas in the path of the fast-moving flames.

The park service forces set to work attempting to hold the southwestern end of the fire and keep it from advancing, concentrating their efforts around the ample water supply at Aunt Betty Pond. Here they set a backfire, a controlled burn, along the inner edge of the fire line to consume the dry understory and parched trees. When the wildfire reached this burned-off swath, it found nothing to burn and changed direction toward the pond. By Thursday morning the wind shifted again, pushing the flames northward and away from Eagle Lake—good news for the Jordan Pond House, which was not threatened again, but creating a precarious situation for the people of the village of Hulls Cove, just outside the park.

The wind blew harder and stronger throughout the day, sending flames directly at the small village of about 250 people, but in the middle of the day it suddenly ceased altogether for a few seconds, and then reversed itself with a roar. A dry cold front had arrived from Canada, changing the wind's direction and increasing its velocity. What had already been a volatile wind of fifty-nine miles per hour accelerated suddenly to gale strength, topping eighty-seven miles per hour. Virtually everything in its path ignited at once, a turn of events for which no one had been prepared. The fire spared Hulls Cove, but it raced southward in front of the northwest wind, moving six miles in just three hours, and headed directly for Bar Harbor and Acadia.

"Even before the flames shot over from Hulls Cove to Bar Harbor, flames . . . came over Great Hill and tore up Cadillac [Mountain] . . . from there striking down the east side of Cadillac to Sieur de Monts Spring," wrote Richard Walden Hale Jr., in his 1949 book, *The Story of Bar Harbor*.

Later that afternoon the Coast Guard would record wind speeds in Penobscot Bay at "between sixty-three and seventy miles an hour," Butler reported in *Wildfire Loose*. In the face of this, much of Bar Harbor burned while some 2,500 of its inhabitants—almost entirely women and children, as most of the men in town had volunteered to help fight the fire—evacuated from their homes to the Athletic Field in the middle of town. When it seemed that the fire could be heading for the field, the entire crowd moved through the evening darkness to the Municipal Pier at the end of Main Street toward the hope of a water rescue. They spread blankets on the ground and waited in the dark on the pier, watching the turbulent waters of Frenchman Bay and hoping beyond hope that they would not have to board small boats and venture out into the churning sea, until word reached them that they had no choice—it was time to leave the island.

Small lobster boats and pleasure craft began to arrive, mostly private craft piloted by people who had heeded the call and hurried to help, bundled up against the October cold and braving the choppy waters whipped up by the fierce wind. Four hundred people steeled themselves and boarded boats that came from Winter Harbor, Gouldsboro, and Lamoine to take them to safety. In the midst of this evacuation, however, the townspeople received word that the fire department had managed to stop the wildfire at the corner of Eden and West Streets. Fire crews used a bulldozer to clear enough still-burning debris from the road to open the way for jeeps, buses, and other vehicles to bring evacuees through the town. By 9:00 p.m., a convoy assembled with as many as seven hundred vehicles, and more than two thousand people were on their way out of town, passing along the edge of the raging flames. Some spotted their own homes burning as they looked back at rows of blazing buildings.

Here in the caravan of vehicles came a further tragedy: the first loss of life during the Bar Harbor fire. "It is difficult to reconstruct just what happened," Butler noted in her book, and the details are indeed slim. Helen Cormier, who was sixteen, and her eleven-year-old sister, Jane, rode in the open back of a US Army truck with about thirty people in total, including their mother, as well as their fox terrier, Tippy, who sat on Jane's lap. Helen had the seat closest to the tailgate. They rode through the worst of the fire with burning embers raining down on them, blocked by a wet tarp they held over their heads.

Just as they found themselves beyond the flames and believed that they were safe on what the *Biddeford Daily Journal* described as "the smoke-shrouded evacuation road," the truck lurched violently and flipped over, throwing its passengers onto the road. Another vehicle had collided with its back wheel.

"We later found out that two officers in the jeep had been drinking, and they rammed the back wheel of our vehicle and knocked it over," Jane told Butler in a recorded interview in 1980, now found on the *Portland Press Herald* website.

The impact threw Helen clear of the truck, but her head hit the pavement and her skull fractured. Jane also fell to the road, but she held tight to Tippy's leash, and the dog dragged her away from the crash site until she was out of danger.

After three days in the hospital in Ellsworth, Helen died of her injury. "The townspeople sympathize with Mr. and Mrs. Cormier in the traffic death of their daughter, Helen," the *Bar Harbor Times* reported on October 30. "Helen was a junior in Bar Harbor High School and active in all its affairs; a great worker in the Girl Reserves and a favorite both with teachers and pupils alike. She will be sorely missed." Her obituary on the same page noted that she had been an honor student.

Helen was not the only person to die from injuries sustained in the crash. Dow Field warrant officer Walter Stephen Coates, who was forty-one and riding in the jeep that collided with the truck, died at the scene. Coates served in World War II, spending a total of thirty-four months overseas and seeing combat in North Africa, Tunisia, Sicily, and southern France. His career with the army spanned eighteen years, and his wife, Gladys, and two children lived with him in Maine while he served at Dow Field.

The fire finally yielded to human control on October 27, though it continued to smolder underground until November 14, when the ordeal officially ended. The devastation in Bar Harbor spread well beyond the loss of lives. "Dozens of mansions burned along 'Millionaire's Row'— today's Route 3 between Bar Harbor and Hulls' Cove [on the shores of Frenchman's Bay]—along with Jackson Lab and many other homes or businesses on the outskirts of town," detailed the *Portland Press Herald* in a retrospective story in 2017. In all, the fire consumed as much as 55 percent of the town, including 170 homes of permanent residents, 67 summer homes owned by wealthy families, and 3 legendary hotels, and brought Mount Desert Island's era as the playground of the rich to an abrupt and dramatic close.

The summer residents did not return to rebuild their estate-like cottages. The fire confirmed what they already knew: with the establishment of the first federal income tax after World War II, their extraordinary incomes were halved, and they could no longer afford such luxuries as a home in Bar Harbor. The skeletons of the burned homes were razed as they sold their land, making way for a line of hotels along Route 3 and a new age of middle-class tourist traffic into the town. Acadia National Park became the central attraction, its visitor numbers increasing with each passing year.

The fire changed the park as well, though, burning more than ten thousand acres and replacing the towering spruce and fir trees with leafy hardwoods including birch, oak, and aspen, the first seeds to find purchase in the newly cleared landscape. Suddenly exposed to sunlight that the tall conifers had blocked, these deciduous trees took hold and grew, now covering Cadillac, Dorr, and other mountains and producing spectacular color displays in the autumn months. Spruce and fir have begun to overtake this successional forest, but it could be many years before the conifers become the dominant trees once again.

With the fire behind it, the park began the slow process of recovery. Park management hired a crew to log some areas of the park, with the combined goals of salvaging what might be useful, cleaning up the carriage roads, and restoring visitor access. The Rockefeller family paid for an additional crew to assist with this. "Some timber was milled, slash was burned, and other logs, still visible today, left to prevent soil erosion," the park's website about the fire tells us. It also reminds readers that fire plays a critical role in a forest's development, by opening areas to species that must have direct sunlight to thrive. The 1947 fire increased the diversity of foliage in the park, a healthy change that provides additional food sources for wildlife.

"The fire on Mount Desert Island was publicized in headlines in newspapers around the world because the island was a renowned summer retreat for the wealthy," the Acadia website concludes. "Statewide, more than 200,000 acres, 851 permanent homes, and 397 seasonal cottages were destroyed in 'the year that Maine burned.'"

## CHAPTER FOURTEEN

# "No Place to Hide"— The Twin Hurricanes of 1954

Affter the hurricane of 1938 turned thousands of people in New England into homeless refugees, devastated Providence, Rhode Island, razed Connecticut's coastline villages, and took the lives of 564 people, the US Weather Bureau sought ways to ensure that no storm of such magnitude could surprise Americans again.

New leadership arrived as Dr. Francis Reichelderfer took the helm at the Weather Bureau. Reichelderfer brought an era of rapid change to the scientific organization, changing processes of forecasting to numerical weather prediction (NWP), a method other weather services around the world regarded with suspicion. The process of NWP uses mathematical models of current weather conditions, calculating the effects of the ocean, atmosphere, and other influences to determine when and how a weather system will develop. Charles Pierce used an early NWP method to make his stunningly accurate prediction of 1938 hurricane's path, raising the Weather Bureau's respect for the potential of equations as a means of forecasting. Not until the 1950s and the arrival of computers did NWP take hold, however—and the first practical use of this technology took place at the Swedish Meteorological and Hydrological Institute in 1954, proving that the process could be used for routine weather prediction.

All the accurate forecasting the Weather Bureau could do would not help, however, if warnings about oncoming storms could not reach residents of the affected area. By the early 1950s, virtually all homes had radios, and many families had made their first investments in black-and-white television sets. Interruptions of programming with breaking news reached most households—a phenomenon so novel that people actually stopped what they were doing and paid attention to what the news bulletin had to say.

So when weather forecasters observed on August 31, 1954, that Hurricane Carol, a Category 3 tropical cyclone by today's measurements, had veered north-northeast after grazing Cape Hatteras, North Carolina, and appeared to be headed for the eastern tip of Long Island at thirty-nine miles per hour, warnings went out over the airwaves along the coast all the way to Cape Cod, Massachusetts. Adults who remembered the hurricane of 1938 bundled their most treasured belongings and their children into their automobiles and evacuated coastal towns by the thousands. More than twenty thousand people left Cape Cod on Route 6, the peninsula's main highway, while residents of Connecticut's shoreline and most of Rhode Island scrambled to get out of the path of the oncoming storm.

In Fairfield Beach, Connecticut, where coastal flooding the previous November had forced residents to evacuate, the community had installed an alert siren to warn seaside families of impending emergencies. Police sounded the siren and cruised in their vehicles up and down Fairfield Beach Road in advance of the hurricane, urging families to get out of the area as quickly as they could—and not a moment too soon. The storm surge arrived with driving force, sweeping across the beach, and flooding homes that had been inhabited hours before. "The water level in some places exceeded the high mark of last November's flood," reported Jules Sebestyen in the *Bridgeport Telegram* on September 1. "A number of residents without cars were evacuated by town trucks and the Red Cross Motor corps." Police officers Philip Ganger and Ambrose Smith took their own lives in their hands to rescue the elderly Mrs. Frederick Marberg from her home, wading through water two feet deep to reach her and carry her to safety. The seventy or so residents took shelter at the Child Memorial parish house, where the Red Cross established an emergency refuge.

Not everyone heard the warnings or took them seriously, however. Many residents in Fairfield County awakened in the wee hours of August 31 as the wind shrieked past their homes, only to discover their ground floors awash in seawater and their car engines waterlogged beneath the rising water's surface. With tidewaters already too high to wade through, shore dwellers found themselves trapped in place, sentenced to a difficult night in the attic if they had one, or a desperate plea for help from the many rescuers in small boats that had mobilized when they received the weather forecast. Police, civil defense workers, and volunteers launched their rowboats and small motorboats and began to round up everyone they could locate as soon as the storm dissipated enough to allow them to move safely.

"Casualties of the storm included autos stalled in flooded streets and abandoned by their owners, boats swamped, overturned or battered against the beach by the raging surf and television antennas twisted grotesquely or knocked down by the lashing winds," the *Bridgeport Telegram* reported on September 1, the day after the storm.

Residents and tourists on normally quiet Block Island found themselves in the direct path of the hurricane, doing their best to hunker down and hang on as the fast-moving system passed over them, registering wind gusts as high as 135 miles per hour.

Hurricane Carol differed significantly from her violent predecessor that had done such damage sixteen years earlier. Equally powerful but smaller, its destructive impact centered on the eastern end of New England as it made landfall in Old Saybrook, Connecticut, and proceeded up the coast. Western Connecticut did not experience the screeching winds and storm surge that pulled apart the coastal towns and cities to the east.

Crossing Long Island Sound only helped the hurricane retain its strength, bringing eighty to one hundred mile-per-hour winds to eastern Connecticut, Rhode Island, and eastern Massachusetts. A storm surge nearly as great as the 1938 storm's extraordinary high tide quickly engulfed downtown Providence once again, this time pushing Narragansett Bay to a height of twelve feet in one-quarter of the city's streets. Groton, Mystic, and New London, Connecticut, could not withstand the deluge that stripped their coastal communities of their homes and cottages. At the base of Cape Cod, Buzzards Bay saw one of the highest surges of its recorded history, stranding people on islands in the bay who did not have mass communications and had no warning of the approaching storm. The one saving grace was the storm's rapid pace, moving so quickly over the area that it did not have time to deposit a great deal of rain. Just two to five inches fell in most areas, with New London receiving six inches, the most of any affected community.

As the storm began to whip eastern Connecticut, Stephen Kopachevsky, a Lincoln Avenue homeowner in Norwich, made one last dash outside to attempt to bring in his lawn furniture before the gale whisked it away. His young son followed him to help, but as they tried to wrest the lawn chairs out of the wind's grasp, a particularly strong gust whipped through a nearby tree and brought it crashing to the ground. Kopachevsky saw the threat to his son's life and reacted quickly, shoving the child out of the way of the falling trunk—but the move placed him directly in the tree's path. In seconds, he found himself pinned to the ground beneath the big tree, unable to move.

Hours later, when the storm abated enough for his family to run for help to get him out from under the tree, Kopachevsky knew that he had sustained serious injuries. He accepted an ambulance ride to William Backus Hospital, where an examination revealed fractures of his skull and back, and a concussion. He was resting quietly in fair condition on the evening of September 1 and was expected to recover.

Not everyone was fortunate enough to survive the storm. In Worcester, Massachusetts, Harry R. Davis, a trustee of the R. C. Taylor Trust, went out to the fire escape of the downtown Medical Arts Building, which the Trust owned, in the midst of the gale. He intended to inspect some repair work that had been completed on the building's tenth story in anticipation of the storm, but he apparently misjudged the severity of the wind and rain at that point. A seventy-mile-per-hour gust seized him and tossed him over the iron railing. He fell more than one hundred feet to Pleasant Street, and died on impact.

Others enjoyed strokes of good luck minutes before their lives could have ended. Mrs. Stanley Gura of Meriden, a young mother with three children, lifted her baby onto her shoulder as seawater flooded her living room on Coral Sands Beach and rose to her waist. Meanwhile, her two young daughters attempted to escape the flooding and go for help by climbing into their rowboat and cutting it loose, but the roiling waters and high winds soon proved too much for them, and they tossed about in their boat like rubber ducks in turbulent bathwater. They screamed for help as their mother stood helpless, praying that her children would somehow emerge safely.

Crescent Beach, Connecticut, took the brunt of the storm surge as Hurricane Carol arrived. (Courtesy NOAA)

To their good fortune, firemen aboard the Essex Fire Duck amphibious boat happened to be nearby, helping to evacuate cottage tenants who had not heeded the storm warnings and moved inland. They heard the girls' frightened screams and turned the boat toward them, rushing to the Gura cottage to help. The firemen steadied the children's rowboat and helped them into the more stable duck boat, all while the girls clamored for them to go into the house and rescue their mother and her baby. Minutes later, the entire Gura family sat in the duck as it motored away through the storm.

"The last thing I saw," Mrs. Gura told the *Hartford Courant*, "was my good chair floating out the door. We put our savings into building that cottage. We shouldn't have done it."

The firemen would not have argued with that conclusion. Each wore a life preserver and had to work hard to keep the duck from flipping over in the violent waves. "We thought we might capsize," one of them told the *Courant*. "It was the roughest weather we ever had her out in."

"Many autos were stalled or abandoned by their owners when they were unable to negotiate the deep water which was reported in many sections of the shore line to have reached a depth of more than five feet," wrote Bob Ward for the *Telegram* on September 1. "Veterans of previous storms reported the tide waters were the highest they had ever seen." More than three hundred people had been evacuated from the low shore areas in Milford, Ward noted, and "countless others were reported to have left their homes of their own accord before the storm struck." As people returned to their homes, "activity along the shore took on a familiar pattern for residents who have experienced this before. Everybody was mopping up and cleaning debris from their homes and yards."

New Englanders who had been chided for not being "hurricane-minded" in 1938 now behaved like seasoned veterans, heeding the warnings of the US Weather Bureau and public service officials and taking responsibility for protecting their lives and property. While some still found themselves in precarious circumstances as they braced for the oncoming storm, most took steps to avoid injury or death, understanding that caution was a requisite of living on the scenic but tempestuous coastline.

Hurricane Carol maintained its brisk speed until it reached New Hampshire and pushed on into Canada, quickly blowing itself out over the mainland in Quebec. The carnage it left in its wake would take days to sort out and much longer to repair, as the Associated Press noted in its September 1 report from Boston. "Damage estimates ran into millions of dollars as summer homes were smashed to kindling, hundreds of yachts were splintered on rocks and shore and power service was severed completely in at least 33 communities," the report said, the first attempt to quantify the extensive destruction. "Most of the storm stricken communities were declared disaster areas and the Red Cross dispatched all-out aid—food, shelter and know-how—to centers in battered Rhode Island, Massachusetts and Connecticut."

In Milford, town manager John J. Desmond toured the affected areas in a police radio car with police superintendent Arthur Harris and quickly sized up the problem spots, dispatching crews with bulldozers, loaders, and trucks to clear the piles of sand, silt, and tree limbs from roads. By the evening of September 1, the biggest snags were gone, and residents made their way back to their homes to assess the damage to their own property.

Evacuees returned to what was left of their homes, and officials began to total up the damages, knowing that the cost of the hurricane would stagger the region. Thirty-two people were dead in New England: seventeen in Rhode Island, seven in Massachusetts, three in New Hampshire, three in Maine, and one each in Vermont and Connecticut—a fraction of the lives lost in 1938, but more than any community wishes to bear. More than 3,000 boats and 3,500 motor vehicles had been dashed to pieces or soaked in salt water until they would never move again. Four thousand families lost their homes. The damages, officials said, would amount to somewhere around $460 million in 1954 dollars—or about $4.3 billion today.

In contrast to the storm to which all other storms were compared, however, much of the damage resulted in fairly minor and temporary inconveniences. Electrical power, crippled by trees falling into power lines, failed in Bridgeport, Stratford, Fairfield, Easton, Trumbull, and Milford, Connecticut, leaving eleven thousand homes without light, heat, or communication. A massive effort to restore power by the United Illuminating Company had more than half of these homes switched back on by the evening of August 31, shortly after the storm moved on. Fallen trees and limbs blocked highways as far west as Greenwich, where a bridge on U.S. Route 1 washed out when the Mianus River spilled over its banks.

The New Haven Railroad in southern Connecticut came to an abrupt halt as seawater flowed over the tracks, dragging debris five feet high onto the rails, and leaving as many as two thousand passengers stranded for several hours. "We have battered boats and cottages, driftwood, stones and sand to a depth of as much as five feet over the trackage between Mystic and Stonington," an unnamed railroad company spokesperson told the *Hartford Courant*. Plus, "the ballast and shoulders of the roadbed have been washed away in a great many places. It will be impossible to move trains over this section of the right of way until the debris has been removed and the roadbed repaired."

The railroad organized a fleet of buses to rescue the riders and take them to Providence if they were traveling east or New London if they were headed west, where they were able to continue to their intended destinations. The New Haven line represented only part of the railroad's challenges that day, the spokesperson continued, noting that a lack of ability to communicate with the line in Cape Cod and along the Connecticut shoreline made it difficult to assess just how much damage their might be in both areas. He did know that the railroad had lost a wooden trestle at Ware, Massachusetts, and that their warehouse at Fall River had taken on quite a bit of floodwater.

While most communities and systems had the ability to resume normal functions in a few days, however, Rhode Island became the major exception. The Associated Press reported on September 1, the day after the storm, that hurricane Carol "outdid in many towns the destructiveness of the disastrous 1938 storm." Nine people had already been reported dead on August 31, and officials predicted the death toll would continue to rise as emergency crews made their way into areas isolated by storm damage.

Warwick, wedged between Greenwich Bay and the Providence River on the shores of Narragansett Bay, suffered a terrible blow as ninety-mile-per-hour winds and the surge-driven high tide tore through the city, leaving buildings shattered and trees ripped from the ground. Town officials declared martial law to prevent further damage from looters, and to keep sightseers and curious residents of other towns from complicating rescue efforts. First responders reached Oakland Beach and discovered the bodies of Catherine Gallo, seventy-two, and her husband, Francesco, under the wreckage of their summer cottage. The body of their thirty-four-year-old nephew, John W. Beland, turned up soon after in a boat that had capsized in the storm surge. Other attempts to escape in boats turned out to be fatal as well: Richard Marsland, forty-seven, drowned in a boat at Oakland Beach, and Pauline J. Hertel drowned while she and her husband, Fred, tried to tie up their boat across the bay from Warwick. Fred managed to escape with a leg fracture, and rescuers took him to a hospital in Providence for treatment.

In the southernmost part of the state, just over the border with Connecticut, Westerly's Misquamicut State Beach took an especially hard beating, just as it had in 1938, "sweeping away more than 200 summer cottages and leaving only two buildings standing," the *Courant* said. So many trees fell across the state that the Narragansett Electric Company simply shut down entirely until work crews could clear the trees and other wreckage enough to work on the lines. "Power work crews were being rushed from as far away as Pittsburgh [Pennsylvania] to aid harried local workmen," the *Courant* reported. "Officials estimated that the storm and flood damage to the Warwick area will prove much greater than that suffered in the 1938 hurricane."

The reports from Cape Cod, Massachusetts, rivaled Rhode Island for widespread destruction. Twenty thousand people had heeded the warnings on radio and television and from their local fire departments and evacuated the coastline ahead of the storm, but this could not save their homes and summer cottages. When the hurricane winds drove the high tide twenty feet above its normal height in New Bedford and Buzzards Bay, more than one thousand cottages collapsed under the weight. "Armed troops patrolled darkened streets of some Cape Cod towns as evacuees slept in public buildings and at homes of the more fortunate," the *North Adams Transcript* reported the day after the storm. While affected residents slept, National Guardsmen kept thieves from plundering their splintered homes in a night devoid of electric light, and spent the following day blocking rubberneckers from wandering the streets and beaches and getting in the way of workers repairing utility lines.

The damage affected millions of people who were without electricity or telephone service for a day or more, but for the most part, New Englanders sensitized to violent storms picked up the pieces and moved forward. If history was any indication, it could be a decade or more before destructive force of this magnitude visited their shores again—and each experience taught them something more about the best ways to prepare for such an eventuality. Normalcy would return, coastal dwellers would rebuild and move on, and life would continue as it always had along the Atlantic and Long Island Sound coasts.

Hurricane Carol pummeled the Connecticut coastline. (Courtesy NOAA)

But not this time.

Eleven days after Hurricane Carol headed northward into Canada, forecasters notified the weather bureau in New England that Hurricane Edna appeared to be heading directly for the Connecticut, Rhode Island, and Massachusetts coast.

Connecticut civil defense director William Hesketh informed first responders and the media that tides from Edna were "expected to be much higher than Carol's," a warning that even the hardiest shoreline residents took to heart. The Connecticut coast cleared out early on the evening of September 10, with residents and vacationers packing up their valuables and enough clothing and supplies for several days. "Residents of the waterfront area were invited over loudspeakers to use . . . evacuation centers, but police reported most of the families appeared to be spending the night with friends inland," the *Boston Globe* reported early on the morning of September 11.

"Civil Defense units were ordered onto an emergency basis earlier by Gov. John Lodge," the *Globe* continued in its coverage of the Connecticut evacuation. "State Police immediately canceled all leaves and ordered emergency equipment and additional Troopers into threatened towns. Selectmen remained up all night to maintain continuous radio contact with police and Civil Defense officials. Military trucks were ordered into the shore communities to help evacuate residents." In New London, where Hurricane Carol had inflicted more than $1 million in damage, residents lost no time in driving away from their waterfront property. The *Globe* noted that by 9:00 p.m. on September 10, coastline communities stood empty.

Even theaters, where "the show must go on" had been a mantra for centuries, shut down operations in preparation for the oncoming storm. The Oakdale Tent Theatre in Wallingford, Connecticut, had taken considerable damage when Hurricane Carol blew through the previous week. This time, it lowered its 110 x 140-foot tent onto its 1,500 seats and canceled its September 10 performance, announcing that a replacement performance would be scheduled for Monday night, September 13. "We can be ready to go in half an hour," a theater spokesperson told the *Globe*.

In Providence, merchants who had barely restocked their shelves after their losses during the last storm began moving their goods upstairs into second floors and above, hoping to avoid the crushing losses Hurricane Carol had caused. The city police chief, John Murphy, ordered all cars removed from downtown Providence from midnight until noon on September 11, and the employees of the Narragansett Electric Company spent the day before the storm piling sandbags ten feet high against the brand-new windows installed just a few days earlier. They braced heavy timbers against the steel outer doors and barricaded themselves inside, ready to respond if the power lines went down throughout the state once again.

Across Rhode Island and eastern Massachusetts, fire departments and Red Cross workers set up shelters in public buildings, stocking them with food, medical supplies, cots, and everything else they now knew they needed to house evacuees from coastal areas for several days. Mobile kitchens to feed emergency workers moved out into the community to the coastal areas where they would most likely be required. Police and firefighters maintained constant communication, watching the forecasts coming in from the weather bureau and sharing all the information they had as Edna moved closer. Gas-powered generators were moved into place to keep essential services, including hospitals, supplied with power.

At Quonset Point Naval Air Station in Rhode Island, pilots evacuated aircraft to inland bases, and all the rolling stock—trailers, trucks, and six huge generators—got transported to higher ground. "As a precautionary measure, however, all Naval ships, which are normally nested at piers, were moved apart and held with separate moorings," the *Boston Globe* reported early on the morning of September 11.

On popular Martha's Vineyard, an island off the coast of Hyannis, Massachusetts, accessed only by ferry, "there is no place to hide," the *Globe* observed. About 6,500 people lived on the island, "plus a few late Summer residents and early arrival for the stripped [*sic*] bass derby." The *Islander*, the high-capacity ferry that could carry more than five hundred people and many automobiles in a single trip, had taken significant damage to its hull when Hurricane Carol blew through, and now operated with a large patch on one side. "Fears rose tonight that the vessel might be crippled by the new storm and unable to make its usual runs tomorrow with food and mail," the *Globe* noted. Even with this fairly strong possibility, however, one island resident told a *Globe* reporter, "There is no hysteria. It's not that we're used to hurricanes, but we're ready for this one, as ready as we can be with what we have."

Weather forecasters believed that the island's most northeastern points at Oak Bluffs and Tisbury stood directly in the storm's path, so state police drove "through a clinging mist" to the homes in these areas to warn residents personally. "During the day residents, just recovering from the pounding given the Vineyard by hurricane Carol, started boarding up windows and bulwarking storm-damaged roads between Vineyard Haven, Oak Bluffs and Edgartown," the *Globe* said. "Along the road between Vineyard Haven and Oak Bluffs, bulldozers attempted to build up a barrier of sand dunes. . . . Some 40 families evacuated north shore homes before 9 tonight to escape the battering expected." As the storm approached, the island's fire department climbed into their trucks and began cruising the roads, with plans to continue to do so all night and into the morning as the storm moved in. If downed power lines sparked fires anywhere in the towns, firefighters would be there in minutes to control and extinguish the blaze.

Thirty miles farther out in the Atlantic, residents of Nantucket were "not taking any extra special precautions," police sergeant Stewart Chadwick told the media. "We're sort of buttoning things up all over." Families on the most exposed island points moved closer to the center of the island to wait out the storm, but for the most part, residents chose to wait until they heard seven blasts of the island's fire whistle, notification that the hurricane had passed through Long Island and was coming toward them. The 3,500 residents and roughly 5,000 summer folk spent September 10 pulling their pleasure boats out of the water and securing them farther inland. "We'll be all right," Chadwick said. "We've had a pretty fair warning on this one."

Connecticut, Rhode Island, and Massachusetts were ready. Hurricane Edna, however, had other ideas about where and how it would make landfall.

The eye of the hurricane passed between Martha's Vineyard and Nantucket at 2:30 p.m. on September 11, delivering winds as high as 120 miles per hour—but it reached the islands at low tide, so it did not produce a major storm surge. As it passed the islands, however, it did something New Englanders had not experienced before: The eye split into two weather systems as it approached Cape Cod. One passed over Brewster on the Inner Cape, while the other proceeded to the Outer Cape and passed northeast of Provincetown. The one farther north moved rapidly up the coast to deliver a stinging slap to Maine, traveling all the way up to Bar Harbor, while the lower segment faltered, sending high water but little wind into southern Massachusetts.

The Coast Guard put in a long day evacuating families in Exeter, New Hampshire, when a dam on the Exeter River looked as if it might give way. While crews worked to reinforce the dam with hundreds of sandbags, Coast Guardsmen used an amphibious vehicle to gather two hundred families from homes and cottages in a low-lying area and bring them to safer ground beyond the river. The sandbags did their job and the dam held, averting what could have been a disastrous situation.

As the storm made its way up the coast and it became clear that Maine would see the worst of it, public officials issued stay-at-home orders to communities, and fire officials in Portland, Maine, shut off the electrical current to overhead circuits before the wind and rain arrived, minimizing the potential danger from loose and broken wires. Repair crews stood at the ready, preparing to mobilize as soon as the worst of the storm had passed.

The additional precautions turned out to be critically important. When Edna arrived in Maine, the scene rivaled the landscape Rhode Island had witnessed less than two weeks earlier. The Kennebec River swelled as the storm let loose eight inches of rain, and soon crested its banks, rising 20.5 feet above its normal level—five feet higher than it usually reached during spring runoff season. In Portland, chunks of highway and railroad track came loose and drifted away, turning up miles from their origins. "Crops lay like a jagged wound today across territory raked by death-dealing hurricane Edna from Massachusetts to Nova Scotia," the Associated Press reported on the evening of September 11. "The death toll reached 20—13 in New England including 8 in Maine, where autos were trapped in road and bridge washouts by streams that went wild under a record eight inches rain." The recovery process added another New England death, bringing the total to 21.

Mr. and Mrs. Fred Brockway of Unity, Maine, and their eight children became trapped in their vehicle as Sandy Stream, normally a small waterway, overflowed and rose rapidly around the car on the nearby road. When it became clear that the water would rise and flood the inside of the car, the family of ten climbed out the windows and crowded onto the car's roof as the rain continued to pour over them. Emergency responders spotted them and moved quickly to help, but it soon became clear that there were few options available with water rushing past the car, even if the fire department had had an amphibious vehicle available to them. They gathered personnel and formed a human chain from the higher ground to the stranded family and began to retrieve the family members one at a time from the roof.

This daring procedure went well for nearly seven hours as the rescuers dodged chunks of debris floating toward them, but as they worked to help eight-year-old Ruth Elaine Brockway reach safety, a particularly large piece of flotsam rammed its way through the human chain. The chain broke, sending Ruth and assistant fire chief Alton L. McCormick, forty-seven, downstream in the swift current. The others could do nothing to rescue them as the child and the chief disappeared from view. Both of them drowned.

The widespread damage went beyond loss of life. Maine racked up $25 million in property damage, on top of $5 million in property and $10 million in ruined crops from Hurricane Carol, making the season the costliest in the state's history (a total of $373 million in today's dollars). New Hampshire saw $5.5 million in Edna damage, in addition to the $5 million it sustained during Carol ($98 million today). Massachusetts took a staggering hit during Carol, sustaining $180 million in damages, and piled on an additional $7.5 million in the second storm ($1.7 billion today). Rhode Island's destruction from Carol amounted to $201 million, with a seemingly paltry $2 million in Edna damage ($1.8 billion). Connecticut saw a $50 million bill for repairs ($466 million today) after Carol, but escaped Edna with minimal additional issues.

Two days after Edna, the federal Civil Defense Administration made an onsite survey of the affected region and declared Maine, Massachusetts, and Rhode Island major disaster areas. Administrator Val Peterson described the damage as "tremendous," and agreed with the governors of the states that their request for financial aid was "reasonable. . . . There is no question, as I understand it, but what Maine took the brunt of Hurricane Edna." He added that President Dwight Eisenhower had "watched the hurricane situation with a great deal of interest and anxiety. The White House was on our telephone in Civil Defense headquarters quite a bit to see that all was being done that could be done."

This was welcome news to each of the states, as "weary utility crews labored to complete repairs to broken electric and telephone lines snapped by Hurricane Edna's eighty-mile-an-hour winds," according to the *Lewiston Daily Sun*. The news of losses to the agriculture industry continued to mount even as Eisenhower signed the disaster area declaration: Maine's apple, oat, potato, and corn crops took a heavy beating, with corn chalked up as a total loss. The state ordered the closing of the Kennebec River to traffic because a boom had broken in Waterville, depositing more than $1 million in paper company Hollingsworth & Whitney's pulpwood into the river, "some of which floated 50 miles to the sea." Hollingsworth & Whitney joined with Hudson Pulp & Paper Company to extend an invitation to residents of Maine to help them in salvaging the logs, offering five dollars per cord of wood collected below Farmingdale.

Slowly, people began to filter back to their own homes to survey the damage. Thirteen New Englanders had perished in the storm—eight of them in Maine—and hundreds found no house where their home had stood days before.

"It looks like Venice," said Mrs. Albert Craig of Portland, the Lewiston paper reported. "There were even whitecaps in the street."

Remarkably and with characteristic New England resiliency, people began picking up the pieces, searching for whatever remnants of their lives lay under the rubble, and rebuilding. Some gathered up what they could and moved on, choosing to relocate further inland. Others constructed new houses on their coastline property, some with built-in precautions to keep the next hurricane—there will always be another hurricane—from wiping their pinpoint off the map.

The 1954 hurricane season produced some positives as well. The US Weather Bureau launched the National Hurricane Research Project, an effort to gain a more comprehensive understanding of hurricanes, how they form, and how the bureau might improve its forecasts of storm strength and intensity. The work of this project team and the subsequent National Hurricane Research Laboratory fueled the move to computer modeling in the 1960s, bringing statistical accuracy to the bureau's predictions. Hurricanes continue to pound the nation's East Coast on an annual basis, but residents receive considerable advance warning of their approach, giving them the opportunity to gauge the need to shelter in place or make a full-scale evacuation.

New Englanders have seen sandy coastlines, old-growth forests, and entire neighborhoods vanish in the face of increasingly severe storms, but they soldier on, treasuring the benefits of expansive ocean views and acknowledging that they occasionally erupt with brutal force. Just as their ancestors braved the wild coastline in the early 1600s, rebuilt their communities after nineteenth- and twentieth-century fires, and sweltered in unprecedented heat in the early 1900s, New England residents continue to see supreme value in living in this spectacular region. Sea levels may rise, and storms may increase in frequency, but New Englanders will undoubtedly choose to stay put for many generations to come.

# Epilogue

Much has changed in the realm of major disasters since the first half of the twentieth century. We no longer rely on the coats of wooly bear caterpillars or the size and quantity of nuts on walnut and hickory trees to help us predict what the weather will be like months down the road. Weather forecasting now allows us to watch a storm's approach in real time from the comfort of our living rooms, vehicles, or desktops, thanks to the invention of Doppler radar and the wonder of the internet. Never again will a hurricane or blizzard— now referred to by NOAA as a "bomb cyclone"—take us completely unaware, as the Long Island Express did back in 1938. Weather alerts erupt on our smartphones hours or even days in advance of the kind of dangerous system that can result in major human losses. Wall-to-wall news coverage warns us of the "storm of the century," "snowpocalypse," or "scorcher" on the horizon, and tells us all we need to know about the impact of major storms and other disasters. We can watch other communities coming apart in real time in the face of weather events and know exactly what to expect from such catastrophes headed our way.

Few of us harbor allusions about waiting out a Category 3 or higher hurricane aimed right for our door. For the most part, with the exception of a few stubborn souls, we evacuate when ordered to do so, or we secure our homes, cars, and watercraft and wait out the worst when "sheltering in place" looks like the better option.

With so much information available, it seems that we should be in less danger than ever before, but this is not really the case. Major weather events have increased in frequency dramatically because of climate change, bringing more tropical storms than ever before to the shores of New England states. What we used to call "one hundred-year storms" now arrive along the United States' East Coast every few years, bringing record-setting winds, large amounts of rainfall and widespread damage.

Only a few of these make their way up the coast to New England, but they do so once a decade—or more often—instead of once a century.

The modern climate trends create other kinds of potential for disasters. New England rarely experiences droughts like the one in 1947 that sparked so many fires, but intensely hot summers and abnormally dry weather affected the region as recently as 2012. Major flood events drenched New Hampshire in 2005, both New Hampshire and Massachusetts in 2006, Rhode Island in 2010, and Vermont in 2011, and heavier annual snowfall in any year can create the potential for more widespread flooding in late winter and early spring.

Happily, modern mitigation methods have protected New England from some of the deconstruction it experienced in the latter half of the nineteenth and first half of the twentieth centuries. Floodwalls and dikes help keep rivers back during high water events, and hurricane protection barriers hold off storm surges. Changes in stream channels help these waterways to allow overflows to pass without breaching their banks. Dams and reservoirs allow water authorities to control the flow, keeping waters literally at bay.

Utilities, however, remain vulnerable to weather events of many kinds, not the least of which include blizzards and ice storms. It remains possible for millions of New England citizens to find themselves without electrical power in the midst of a winter storm, a situation that will require major infrastructure updates to rectify. Four such events took place in the first three weeks of March 2018 alone, with high winds and heavy snows that resulted in power outages.

After reading the stories of disasters in this book, you may feel grateful that you live in an era of plentiful weather information and mass communication, when you are not likely to experience the kinds of devastating losses literally millions of New Englanders suffered before meteorology's current golden age. We are indeed lucky to live in a time when we can count on surviving whatever nature throws at us because we know it's coming, and we take every precaution to limit the impact on our daily lives. We sweep up the debris, chop and stack our downed trees for firewood, make repairs, and continue on our way.

The fact is, however, that we will see more extreme weather events over the next decade and beyond as climate change accelerates. No amount of warning can fully protect us from more frequent storms and other weather events, as climate change upsets the balance of New England's ecosystems.

The stories contained in this book are a selection of the most interesting New England disasters—that is, the ones about which there is enough information to tell a good story. These are far from the only fascinating tales in the region's history, of course, so if there is another disaster you would like to see explored, please let me know at author@minetor.com, or on Facebook for Nic's and my books, @minetorbooks. We'd love to hear from you and keep the conversation going.

In the meantime, watch the water, dress warmly, stay out of the wind, and when people who know what's coming tell you to evacuate, get the heck out of there.

# Sources

## INTRODUCTION

Kinzel, Bob. "Road Repairs Will Top $700 Million, But Federal Aid Uncertain." Vermont Public Radio, Sept. 27, 2011, accessed Dec. 10, 2019. archive.vpr.org/vpr-news/road-repairs-will-top-700-million-but-federal -aid-uncertain/.

Minetor, Randi. "Rural Vermont Gets a Jewel Box." PLSN, Nov. 9, 2017. Accessed Dec. 10, 2019. plsn.com/articles/venue-design/rural-vermont -gets-a-jewel-box-weston-playhouse-at-walker-farm/.

Pierre-Lewis, Kendra. "Five Years After Hurricane Irene, Vermont Still Striving for Resilience." InsideClimate News, Sept. 1, 2016, accessed Dec. 10, 2019. insideclimatenews.org/news/31082016/five-years-after-hurricane -irene-2011-effects-flooding-vermont-damage-resilience-climate-change.

## CHAPTER 1

Bradford, William. *Bradford's History "Of Plimouth Plantation."* Boston: Wright & Potter Printing Co., 1899, pp. 401–02.

"Captain Robert Andrews." Rootsweb, accessed Oct. 7, 2019. freepages.roots web.com/~rothlisberger/genealogy/rothlisberger/996.htm.

"History of the National Weather Service." National Weather Service, National Oceanic and Atmospheric Administration, accessed Oct. 2, 2019. weather .gov/timeline.

Mather, Richard. *Collections of the Dorchester Antiquarian and Historical Society Number Three: Journal of Richard Mather 1635. His Life and Death 1670.* Boston: David Clapp & Sons, 1850, pp. 29–31.

Prater, Lisa Foust. "Old Wives' Tales Predict Winter Weather." *Living the Country Life*, Oct. 25, 2018, accessed Oct. 2, 2019.

"Red Sky at Night and Other Weather Lore. "Met Office, accessed Oct. 2, 2019. metoffice.gov.uk/weather/learn-about/weather/how-weather-works/ red-sky-at-night.

"The Sky an Indicator of the Weather . . ." *Evening Star*, Washington, DC, Jan. 26, 1860, p. 1. Accessed Oct. 7, 2019. newspapers.com/image/168071547/ ?terms=weather.

Winthrop, John. *Winthrop's Journal, "History of New England," 1630–1649.* Hosmer, James Kendall, ed. New York: Charles Scribner's Sons, 1908, pp. 155–57.

## CHAPTER 2

Adams, Eliphalet. "A discourse occasioned by the late distressing storm which began Feb. 20th, 1716.17. As it was deliver'd March 3d, 1716." Evans Early American Imprint Collection, Text Creation Partnership, accessed Oct. 29, 2019. quod.lib.umich.edu/e/evans/N01568.0001.001/1:2?rgn=div1 ;size=25;start=1;submit=Go;subview=detail;type=simple;view=fulltext ;q1=snow.

Caulkins, Frances Manwaring. *History of New London, Connecticut: From the First Survey of the Coast in 1612 to 1860.* Carlisle, MA: Applewood Books, 2010; originally published 1895.

Cram, William Dow. "The Great Blizzard of 1717." Little Stories of Old New England, *Hampton Union* and *Rockingham County Gazette*, Dec. 1, 1938. Accessed at Lane Memorial Library website, Oct. 29, 2019. hampton.lib .nh.us/hampton/history/oral/Cram/blizzard1717.htm.

Lepore, Jill. "An Horrid Snow." *The New Yorker*, Feb. 1, 2011, accessed Oct. 28, 2019. https://www.newyorker.com/news/news-desk/an-horrid-snow.

Mather, Cotton. "An Horrid Snow," found in Barber, John Warner. The History and Antiquities of New England, New York, New Jersey, and Pennsylvania." C. Allyn, 1856, pp. 476–78.

## CHAPTER 3

"Boston, August 20." *Pennsylvania Gazette*, Aug. 28, 1787, p. 2. Accessed Oct. 29, 2019. newspapers.com/image/41020858/?terms=tornado.

"Boston, August 24." *Vermont Journal*, Sept. 17, 1787, pp. 2–3. Accessed Oct. 29, 2019. newspapers.com/image/488988145/.

"Northampton, August 22." *Vermont Journal*, Aug. 27, 1787, p. 4. Accessed Oct. 29, 2019. newspapers.com/image/488992182/?terms=tornado.

Perley, Sidney. *Historic Storms of New England*. Salem, MA: The Salem Press Publishing and Printing Co., 1891, pp. 135–42.

"Providence, August 18." *The Pennsylvania Packet*, Aug. 29, 1787, p. 3. Accessed Oct. 29, 2019. newspapers.com/image/39433668/?terms=tornado.

Shea, Jim. "Connecticut's Past Checkered with Tornado Deaths." *Hartford Courant*, Jan. 12, 2014.

## CHAPTER 4

Farrar, John. "An account of the violent and destructive storm of the 23d day of September, 1815." *The Quarterly Journal of Literature, Science and the Arts*, Vol. 7. London: John Murray, 1819, pp. 102–06. Accessed Oct. 10, 2019. books.google.com/books?id=HyxGAAAAcAAJ&printsec=front cover&source=gbs_ge_summary_r&cad=0#v=onepage&q&f=false.

Ludlam, David M. *Early American Hurricanes, 1492–1870*. Boston: American Meteorological Society, 1963, pp. 80–81.

"New London, Sept. 27," "Worcester, (Ma.) Sept. 27," and "From the Boston Centinel [*sic*], Sept. 27." *New York Evening Post*, Sept. 28, 1815, p. 2. Accessed Oct. 21, 2019. newspapers.com/image/38139479/?terms= hurricane.

Norcross, Bryan. *Hurricane Almanac: The Essential Guide to Storms Past, Present, and Future*. New York: St. Martin's Press, May 29, 2007, p. 96.

Perley, Sidney. *Historic Storms of New England*. Salem, MA: The Salem Press Publishing and Printing Co., 1891, pp. 187–203.

"Saffir-Simpson Hurricane Wind Scale." National Hurricane Center and Central Pacific Hurricane Center, National Oceanic and Atmospheric Administration.

## CHAPTER 5

"All Sorts of Paragraphs." *Boston Post*, Oct. 20, 1841, p. 2. Accessed Oct. 24, 2019. newspapers.com/image/56422678/?terms=Nantucket%2Bgale.

"All Sorts of Paragraphs." *Boston Post*, Oct. 26, 1841, p. 2. Accessed Oct. 24, 2019. newspapers.com/image/56423192/?terms=Nantucket%2Bgale.

"Disasters &c." *The Boston Post*, Oct. 7, 1841, p. 2. Accessed Oct. 24, 2019. newspapers.com/image/56421726/?terms=Nantucket%2Bgale.

"From Our Correspondents: Hyannis Port, Gloucester." *Boston Post*, Oct. 5, 1841, p. 2. Accessed Oct. 24, 2019. newspapers.com/image/56421661/ ?terms=gale.

"The Gale at Nantucket." *Nantucket Inquirer*, reprinted in *The Boston Post*, Oct. 7, 1841, p. 2. Accessed Oct. 24, 2019. newspapers.com/image/56421726/ ?terms=Nantucket%2Bgale.

Ludlum, David, op. cit., pp. 91–93. "Marine Journal, Disasters, &c." *Boston Post*, Oct. 9, 1841, p. 2. Accessed Oct. 24, 2019. newspapers.com/image/ 56421862/?terms=Nantucket%2Bgale.

"Marine Journal, Disasters &c." *Boston Post*, Oct. 11, 1841, p. 2. Accessed Oct. 24, 2019. newspapers.com/image/56421931/?terms=truro.

"Marine Journal, Disasters &c." *Boston Post*, Oct. 21, 1841, p. 2. Accessed Oct. 24, 2019. newspapers.com/image/56422732/?terms=Nantucket%2Bgale.

"Naval." *Baltimore Sun*, Oct. 15, 1841, p.2. Accessed Oct. 24, 2019. news papers.com/image/364983283/?terms=Nantucket%2Bgale.

Perley, Sidney, op. cit., pp. 279–88.

Wilding, Don. "Shore Lore: Truro and the 'October Gale' of 1841." Wicked Local: Truro, content from the *Provincetown Banner*, Oct. 6, 2017. Accessed Oct. 27, 2019. truro.wickedlocal.com/news/20171006/shore-lore-truro -and-october-gale-of-1841.

## CHAPTER 6

"A Terrible Conflagration, Nantucket in Ruins!" *Fall River Monitor*, July 18, 1846, p. 2. Accessed Oct. 30, 2019. newspapers.com/image/589863089/ ?terms=fire%2BNantucket.

Bunker, James M. "The Late Calamity." *The Warder*, July 18, 1856, p. 1. Accessed Oct. 30, 2019. digital.olivesoftware.com/Olive/APA/Nantucket/ default.aspx#panel=document.

"City Intelligence." *Brooklyn Daily Eagle*, July 24, 1846, p. 2. Accessed Oct. 30, 2019. newspapers.com/image/50242887/?terms=fire%2BNantucket.

"Destructive Fire at Nantucket." *The Liberator*, Boston, July 24, 1856, p. 4. Accessed Oct. 30, 2019. newspapers.com/image/34613195/?terms=fire %2BNantucket.

Editor of the *Nantucket Mirror*, unnamed. "Awful Calamity—One Third of our Town in Ruins." *The Warder*, July 15, 1846, p. 1. Accessed Oct. 30, 2019. digital.olivesoftware.com/Olive/APA/Nantucket/default.aspx#panel =document.

"Fire Nearly Destroys Nantucket Town." MassMoments, accessed Oct. 30, 2019. massmoments.org/moment-details/fire-nearly-destroys-nantucket -town.html.

Fowler, Orin. History of Fall River with notices of Freetown and Tiverton. Original publisher unknown, 1923. Accessed Oct. 31, 2019. sailsinc.org/durfee/fowler5.pdf.

"Great Fire at Nantucket." *Baltimore Sun*, July 17, 1846, p. 1. Accessed Oct. 30, 2019. newspapers.com/image/365250106/?terms=fire%2BNantucket.

"Great Fire at Nantucket." *New York Evening Post*, July 16, 1846, p. 2. Accessed Oct. 30, 2019. newspapers.com/image/39630518/?terms=fire%2BNantucket.

"The Great Fire at Nantucket." *Baltimore Daily Commercial*, Maryland, July 18, 1846, p. 4. Accessed Oct. 30, 2019. newspapers.com/image/325527934/?terms=fire%2BNantucket.

"The Great Fire in Nantucket." *The Liberator*, Boston, July 31, 1856, p. 3. Accessed oct. 30, 2019. newspapers.com/image/34613198/?terms=fire%2BNantucket.

Leland, P. W. "Nantucket and Fall River." *Fall River Monitor*, Mass., Aug. 8, 1846, p. 2. Accessed Oct. 30, 2019. newspapers.com/image/589863148/?terms=fire%2BNantucket.

"Postscript." *Weekly National Intelligencer*, Washington, DC, July 18, 1846, p. 3. Accessed Oct. 30, 2019. newspapers.com/image/334676324/?terms=fire%2BNantucket.

"Terrible Conflagration at Nantucket." *Pittsfield Sun*, July 23, 1846, p. 2. Accessed Octo. 30, 2019. newspapers.com/image/531894256/?terms=fire%2BNantucket.

## CHAPTER 7

Allison, F. "To the Editors of the Express." *Halifax Evening Express*, Nova Scotia, Oct. 1, 1869. Accessed Aug. 24, 2017. web.archive.org/web/20050226162348/http://www.magma.ca/~jdreid/Express.htm.

"By Telegraph: The Flood in the East." *The Daily Kansas Tribune*, Oct. 6, 1869, p. 2. Accessed Aug. 24, 2017. newspapers.com/image/60533244/?terms=J.M.%2BThompson.

"Great Hurricane and Freshet in Maine." *Evening Star*, Washington, DC, Oct. 11, 1869, p. 1. Accessed Oct. 31, 2019. newspapers.com/image/168176790/?terms=Maine%2Bhurricane.

"Hurricane in Maine, Buildings Smashed to Atoms." *Morning Democrat*, Davenport, Iowa, Oct. 11, 1869, p. 1. Accessed Oct. 31, 2019. newspapers.com/image/36958669/?terms=Maine%2Bhurricane.

"The Latest Hurricane." *Philadelphia Inquirer*, Oct. 12, 1869, p. 4. Accessed Oct. 31, 2019. newspapers.com/image/168133833/?terms=Maine%2 Bhurricane.

"Maine: Terrible Hurricane." *Philadelphia Inquirer*, Oct. 11, 1869, p. 1. Accessed Oct. 31, 2019. newspapers.com/image/168132702/?terms= Maine%2Bhurricane.

Minetor, Randi. *Death on Mount Washington: Stories of Accidents and Foolhardiness on the Northeast's Highest Peak*. Guilford, CT: Lyons Press, 2018, pp. 145–47.

Munger, Sean. "The Saxby Gale: A Weather Disaster Predicted, or Just a Lucky Guess?" SeanMunger.com, Oct. 5, 2014. Accessed Aug. 24, 2017. sean munger.com/2014/10/05/the-saxby-gale-a-weather-disaster-predicted-or -just-a-lucky-guess/.

Saxby, S. M., R. N. "To the Editor." *The Standard*, London, England, Dec. 25, 1868. Accessed Aug. 24, 2017. web.archive.org/web/20050226214115/ http://www.magma.ca/~jdreid/saxby25dec.htm.

Saxby, S. M., R. N. "Equinoctal Gales." *The Standard*, London, England, Sept. 16, 1869. Accessed Aug. 24, 2017. web.archive.org/web/20050301170130/ http://www.magma.ca/~jdreid/saxby14sept.htm.

"Storm Signals." *The New Jersey Standard*, Oct. 1, 1869, p. 2. Accessed Oct. 31, 2019. newspapers.com/image/418911417/?terms=Maine%2Bhurricane.

## CHAPTER 8

"The Great Storm." Associated Press, in *The Buffalo Commercial*, March 12, 1888, p. 1. Accessed Nov. 4, 2019. newspapers.com/image/269473387/ ?terms=blizzard.

"Grim Winter. The Great Storm and Boston's Isolation." *Boston Globe*, March 15, 1888, p. 2. Accessed Nov. 2, 2019. newspapers.com/image/430866143/.

"Like a Roaring Lion: New Haven Visited by a Furious Blizzard." *Morning Journal-Courier*, New Haven, Conn., March 13, 1888, p. 2. Accessed Nov. 2, 2019. newspapers.com/image/466094817/?terms=blizzard.

"March's Beginning. Review of the First Week of Spring Weather—How the Recent Storm Was Disrupted." *Boston Globe*, March 9, 1888, p. 5. Accessed Nov. 2, 2019. newspapers.com/image/430865532/?terms= blizzard.

"Silence." *Boston Globe*, March 13, 1888, pp. 1 and 5. Accessed Nov. 5, 2019. newspapers.com/image/430866017/.

"Snow-Bound: Storm Embargo Grows Worse," etc. *Fall River Daily Evening News*, Mass., March 14, 1888, p. 3. Accessed Nov. 6, 2019. newspapers .com/image/590004350/?terms=blizzard.

"Storm-Swept. A Cyclone Swoops Down Upon New York. Gale of Awful Fury Raging." *Boston Globe*, March 12, 1888, p. 1. Accessed Nov. 2, 2019. newspapers.com/image/430865849/.

"The Terrible Storm." *Hartford Courant*, March 13, 1888, p. 1. Accessed Nov. 4, 2019. newspapers.com/image/367339203/?terms=fire%2BStamford.

## CHAPTER 9

"11 Prostrations from the Heat." *Hartford Courant*, July 6, 1911, p. 10. Accessed Nov. 6, 2019. newspapers.com/image/369105450/.

"52 Lose Lives in New England." *The Washington Post*, DC, July 6, 1911, p. 2. Accessed Nov. 14, 2019. newspapers.com/image/19476400/ ?terms=New%2BEngland%2Bheat%2Bwave.

"Break in Hot Wave at Hand." *Hartford Courant*, July 5, 1911, p. 1. Accessed Nov. 6, 2019. newspapers.com/image/369105318/?terms=heat%2Bwave %2BConnecticut.

"Cooler Weather Coming To-night." *Fall River Daily Evening News*, Mass., July 6, 1911, p. 5. Accessed Nov. 14, 2019. newspapers.com/image/590542922/ ?terms=New%2BEngland%2Bheat%2Bwave.

"Downpour Causes Heavy Damage But Brings Relief." *Hartford Courant*, July 7, 1911, p. 1. Accessed Nov. 14, 2019. newspapers.com/image/369105610/ ?terms=New%2BEngland%2Bheat%2Bwave.

"Hard Test for Undertakers." *Boston Globe*, July 8, 1911, p. 2. Accessed Nov. 14, 2019. newspapers.com/image/431180305/.

"Hottest Yet Known in Boston Records." *Boston Globe*, July 4, 1911, p. 1 and 8. Accessed Nov. 13, 2019. newspapers.com/image/431172553/.

"The Hot Wave Breaking at Last." *Norwich Bulletin*, Conn., July 6, 1911, p. 1. Accessed Nov. 6, 2019. newspapers.com/image/319397212/ ?terms=heat%2Bwave%2BConnecticut.

"Lightning All Around Rutland." *Burlington Free Press*, Vermont, July 7, 1911, p. 1. Accessed Nov. 14, 2019. newspapers.com/image/197351474/ ?terms=New%2BEngland%2Bheat%2Bwave.

"New England Sizzles in Awful Heat." *Salt Lake Telegram*, Utah, July 4, 1911, p. 1. Accessed Nov. 13, 2019. newspapers.com/image/289686821/ ?terms=New%2BHampshire%2Bheat.

"One Death From the Heat." *Boston Globe*, July 4, 1911, p. 7. Accessed Nov. 13, 2019. newspapers.com/image/431176427/?terms=Massachusetts%2Bheat.

"Over 500 Deaths Due to Heat." *Rutland Daily Herald*, Vermont, July 6, 1911, p. 1. Accessed Nov. 14, 2019. newspapers.com/image/533719223/?terms=New%2BEngland%2Bheat%2Bwave.

Shea, Jim. "In 1911, Deadly Heat Settles Over Northeast." *Hartford Courant*, Jan. 19, 2014. Accessed Nov. 6, 2019. courant.com/courant-250/moments-in-history/hc-in-1911-deadly-heat-settles-over-northeast-20140117-htmlstory.html.

"Showers Relieve Many Sections." *Norwich Bulletin*, July 7, 1911, p. 1. Accessed Nov. 14, 2019. newspapers.com/image/319397360/?terms=New%2BEngland%2Bheat%2Bwave.

"Showers Will Break Up Hot Wave For us." *Bridgeport Times and Evening Farmer*, Conn., July 5, 1911, p. 1. Accessed Nov. 6, 2019. newspapers.com/image/336139504/.

"Warm Fourth is Forecasted." *Boston Globe*, July 4, 1911, p. 7. Accessed Nov. 13, 2019. newspapers.com/image/431176427/?terms=Massachusetts%2Bheat.

"White Mountain for New Hampshire, Famed For Cool Breezes, Gave No Relief." *Cincinnati Inquirer*, July 4, 1911, p. 2. Accessed Nov. 13, 2019. newspapers.com/image/33336551/?terms=New%2BHampshire%2Bheat.

## CHAPTER 10

"15 Killed, 150 Injured in North End Explosion." *Boston Evening Globe*, Jan. 15, 1919, p. 1, 2. Accessed Nov. 19, 2019. newspapers.com/image/431228635/.

"Death Toll From Tank Disaster 13." *Boston Globe*, Jan. 18, 1919, pp. 1, 3. Accessed Nov. 20, 2019. newspapers.com/image/430831725/.

"Molasses Tank Explosion Injures 50 and Kills 11." *Boston Globe*, Jan. 16, 1919, p. 1, 7, 8. Accessed Nov. 15, 2019. newspapers.com/image/430831009/.

Puleo, Stephen. *Dark Tide: The Great Boston Molasses Flood of 1919*. Boston: Beacon Press, 2003, 2019.

## CHAPTER 11

Applebee, L. K., Jr. "Montpelier's Plight Highly Exaggerated." *Rutland Herald*, Nov. 6, 1927, p. 1. Accessed Nov. 26, 2019. newspapers.com/image/533769795/.

"Bridge Out at Pittsford." *Rutland Daily Herald*, Nov. 5, 1927, p. 1. Accessed Nov. 26, 2019. newspapers.com/image/533769586/.

Bushnell, Mark. "Then Again: Remembering the terror and losses of 1927 flood." VTDigger, Sept. 4, 2016. Accessed Nov. 25, 2019. vtdigger.org/ 2016/09/04/then-again-remembering-the-terror-and-losses-of-1927 -flood/.

"City of Montpelier Asks Burlington To Send Boats." *Burlington Free Press*, Nov. 4, 1927, p. 1. Accessed Nov. 25, 2019. newspapers.com/image/?clipping_ id=37813540&fcfToken=eyJhbGciOiJIUzI1NiIsInR5cCI6IkpXVCJ9. eyJmcmVlLXZpZXctaWQiOjE5NzMyNDU0NSwiaWF0IjoxNTc0ON zAwOTkwLCJleHAiOjE1NzQ3ODczOTB9.lCzUSXBMceSrJR5Ju koMvNzJJQZJNKMRTKLVsHzAuvA.

"Find Jackson's Body Near Home in Barre." *Rutland Daily Herald*, Nov. 6, 1927, p. 1. Accessed Nov. 26, 2019. newspapers.com/image/533769795/.

"Floods Drive Vermont People From Homes—Heavy Property Damage." *Burlington Free Press*, Nov. 4, 1927, p. 1, 2. Accessed Nov. 25, 2019. news papers.com/image/197324545/.

"Floods Sweep City, State." *Rutland Herald*, Nov. 4, 1927, p. 1. Accessed Nov. 25, 2019. newspapers.com/image/533769357/?terms=flood.

"Historic Flood November 1927." National Weather Service, accessed Nov. 25, 2019. weather.gov/nerfc/hf_november_1927.

Kinnison, H. B. "The New England Flood of November, 1927." Contributions to Hydrology of United States, Washington, DC, U.S. Geological Survey, 1929, pp. 45–67. Accessed Nov. 25, 2019. pubs.usgs.gov/wsp/0636c/ report.pdf.

"Mill Swept Away At Bellows Falls." *Rutland Daily Herald*, Nov. 5, 1927, p. 1. Accessed Nov. 26, 2019. newspapers.com/image/533769586/.

"Spend Night Atop Engine." *Rutland Daily Herald*, Nov. 5, 1927, p. 1. Accessed Nov. 26, 2019. newspapers.com/image/533769586/.

## CHAPTER 12

"18 Dead, Hundreds Injured, Damage Millions As Hurricane Lashes Through Connecticut." *Hartford Courant*, Sept. 22, 1938, p. 1, 2. Accessed Nov. 27, 2019. newspapers.com/image/370004999/?terms=hurricane%2B Connecticut.

"Flood Shortage Seen in Norwich." *Hartford Courant*, Sept. 24, 1938, pp. 1, 8. Accessed Dec. 1, 2019. newspapers.com/image/370009469/.

"Glastonbury Sees Building Sailing." *Hartford Courant*, Sept. 22, 1938, p. 1, 20. Accessed Nov. 30, 2019. newspapers.com/image/370005803/.

"The Great New England Hurricane of 1938." Weather.gov, accessed Nov. 27, 2019. weather.gov/okx/1938HurricaneHome.

"The Great New England Hurricane of 1938: History." National Weather Service, accessed Nov. 27, 2019. weather.gov/okx/1938HurricaneHistory.

Grossi, Patricia. "The 1938 Great New England Hurricane: Looking to the Past to Understand Today's Risk." Risk Management Solutions (RMS), Newark, Calif., 2008. Accessed Dec. 2, 2019. forms2.rms.com/rs/729 -DJX-565/images/tc_1938_great_new_england_hurricane.pdf.

"Hartford Moves One More Step Toward Normal." *Hartford Courant*, Oct. 5, 1938, p. 7. Accessed Dec. 2, 2019. newspapers.com/image/370282913/ ?terms=hurricane.

Hepburn, Katharine. *Me: Stories of My Life*. New York, Knopf, 1991.

Lipman, Don. "The Great New England Hurricane of September 21, 1938 on its 75th anniversary." *Washington Post*, Sept. 20, 2013.

"Rehabilitation Ousts Rogers Addition Needs." *Newport Mercury*, Oct. 7, 1938, p. 1. Accessed Dec. 2, 2019. newspapers.com/image/16374944/?terms= hurricane%2BRhode%2BIsland.

*Shock Troops of Disaster*. Work Projects Administration, Federal Works Agency, 1938. youtube.com/watch?v=RpOGTqdeDsE.

"Violent Earth: New England's Killer Hurricane of 1938." History Channel, 2006. Accessed Dec. 1, 2019. youtube.com/watch?v=evxGkUFpV54.

"Wind, Fire and Flood." *Hartford Courant*, Sept. 23, 1938, p. 18. Accessed Nov. 30, 2019. newspapers.com/image/370006580/?terms=hurricane% 2BConnecticut.

Zim. "Katharine Hepburn & the New England Hurricane of 1938." History By Zim, July 24, 2015. Accessed Dec. 1, 2019. historybyzim.com/2015/07/ katharine-hepburn-the-new-england-hurricane-of-1938/.

## CHAPTER 13

"200 Houses Lost in Coastal Area; Looting Starts." *Biddeford Daily Journal*, Oct. 22, 1947, pp. 1, 2. Accessed Dec. 5, 2019. newspaperarchive.com/ biddeford-daily-journal-oct-22-1947-p-1/.

"60 Forest Fires Sweep State; 21 In York County." Associated Press, located in *Biddeford Daily Journal*, Oct. 18, 1947, p. 1. Accessed Dec. 9, 2019. newspaperarchive.com/biddeford-daily-journal-oct-18-1947-p-1/.

Butler, Joyce. "Listen: Survivors describe fleeing and fighting the fires of '47." *Portland Press Herald*, recorded in 1980, posted Oct. 22, 2017, accessed Oct. 9, 2018. pressherald.com/2017/10/22/listen-survivors-describe -fleeing-fighting-fires-47/#cormier.

Butler, Joyce. *Wildfire Loose: The Week Maine Burned.* Camden, ME: Down East Books, 2014 (unabridged reprint of 1997 version).

"Dry Woods Become Serious Fire Hazard in New England." Associated Press, located in *Biddeford Daily Journal*, Oct. 15, 1947, p. 1. Accessed Dec. 9, 2019. newspaperarchive.com/biddeford-daily-journal-oct-15-1947-p-1/.

"Entire Island Menaced by Fire." *Bar Harbor Times*, Oct. 23, 1947, p. 1, accessed Oct. 9, 2018. newspaperarchive.com/bar-harbor-times-oct-23 -1947-p-1/.

"Fire of 1947." Acadia National Park website, National Park Service, accessed Oct. 9, 2018. nps.gov/acad/learn/historyculture/fireof1947.htm.

"Former Resident Dies Fighting Fire in Maine Forest." New Castle, Pa., News, Oct. 27, 1947, p. 9, accessed Oct. 9, 2018. newspaperarchive.com/new -castle-news-oct-27-1947-p-9/.

Hale, Richard Walden, Jr. *The Story of Bar Harbor.* New York: Ives Washburn, Inc., 1949.

"Hildreth Suspends Hunting in Maine Because of Drouth." *Biddeford Daily Journal*, Oct. 16, 1947, p. 1. Accessed Dec. 9, 2019. newspaperarchive. com/biddeford-daily-journal-oct-16-1947-p-1/.

King, James F. "Maine Fire Area Looks Like a Petrified Forest." Associated Press, located in *Biddeford Daily Journal*, Oct. 22, 1947, pp. 1, 2. Accessed Dec. 5, 2019. newspaperarchive.com/biddeford-daily-journal-oct-22 -1947-p-1/.

Letourneau, Gene L. "Sportsmen Say." *Portland Sunday Telegram*, Oct. 19, 1947, p. 7. Accessed Dec. 9, 2019. newspaperarchive.com/portland -sunday-telegram-and-sunday-press-herald-oct-19-1947-p-7/.

"Local fire casualties are all improving." *Bar Harbor Times*, Oct. 30, 1947, p. 5, accessed Oct. 9, 2018. newspaperarchive.com/bar-harbor-times-oct-30 -1947-p-5/.

"Maine May Close Woods Today." Associated Press, located in *Portland Press Herald*, Oct. 16, 1947, p. 1, 19. Accessed Dec. 9, 2019. newspaper archive.com/portland-press-herald-oct-16-1947-p-1/.

Miller, Kevin. "When Maine burned: How the monster Fire of '47 tested the state's resilience and altered its landscape." *Portland Press Herald*, Oct. 28, 2017.

Miller, Kevin. "Fire had profound impact on Bar Harbor and Acadia." *Portland Press Herald*, Oct. 21, 2017.

"New Forest Fires Rage as Woods Ban Becomes Effective." Associated Press, located in *Biddeford Daily Journal*, Oct. 17, 1947, p. 1. Accessed Dec. 9, 2019. newspaperarchive.com/biddeford-daily-journal-oct-17-1947-p-1/.

Patterson, William A., Saunders, Karen E., Horton, L. J. "Fire Regimes of the Coastal Maine Forests of Acadia National Park." US Department of the Interior, National Park Service, North Atlantic Region, Office of Scientific Studies, OSS 83-3, undated (approx. 1980). pp. 6-1 to 6-30. Accessed Oct. 8, 2018. pubs.etic.nps.gov/Etic/ACAD_123_146674_0001_of_0291.pdf.

"Side Lights on Fire." *Biddeford Daily Journal*, Oct. 22, 1947, pp. 1, 2. Accessed Dec. 5, 2019. newspaperarchive.com/biddeford-daily-journal-oct-22-1947-p-1/.

"Ten Woods Fires Rage in Maine." *Portland Press Herald*, Oct. 15, 1947, p. 1. Accessed Dec. 9, 2019. newspaperarchive.com/portland-press-herald-oct-15-1947-p-1/.

"Twenty-Five Homes Burned; Goose Rocks Afire." *Biddeford Daily Journal*, Oct. 21, 1947, p. 1, 2. Accessed Dec. 9, 2019. newspaperarchive.com/biddeford-daily-journal-oct-21-1947-p-1/.

"Two killed when convoys collide." *Biddeford Daily Journal*, Oct. 24, 1947, p. 2, accessed Oct. 9, 2018. newspaperarchive.com/biddeford-daily-journal-oct-24-1947-p-2/.

"Weary Crews Rest as Forest Fires Ease Up." *Portland Press Herald*, Oct. 20, 1947, p. 1. Accessed Dec. 9, 2019. newspaperarchive.com/portland-press-herald-oct-20-1947-p-1/.

"West Falmouth Pastor Calls on People to Pray for Rain Tonight." *Portland Press Herald*, Oct. 20, 1947, p. 1. Accessed Dec. 9, 2019. newspaperarchive.com/portland-press-herald-oct-20-1947-p-1/.

## CHAPTER 14

"19 Left Dead in Wake of Hurricane; Maine Hardest Hit, Calls On Ike." Associated Press, located in *Newport Daily News*, Sept. 11, 1954, p. 1. Accessed Dec. 12, 2019. newspapers.com/image/59294589/?terms=Hurricane%2BEdna.

"1954-Hurricane Carol." Hurricanes: Science and Society, accessed Dec. 11, 2019. hurricanescience.org/history/storms/1950s/carol/.

"32 Killed As Hurricane Rips N.E." *Bridgeport Telegram*, Sept. 1, 1954, p. 1. Accessed Dec. 11, 2019. newspapers.com/image/23028099/.

Cotterly, Wayne. "Hurricane Edna." Maine Hurricane History, Oct. 21, 2002, accessed via Internet Archive, Dec. 13, 2019. web.archive.org/web/20070222045854/http://www.pivot.net/~cotterly/edna.htm.

"Edna Due to Hit N.E. at 9." *Boston Globe*, Sept. 11, 1954, p. 1, 10. Accessed Dec. 12, 2019. newspapers.com/image/433376530/.

"Edna Leaves Floods In Her Wake." *Portsmouth Herald*, New Hampshire, Sept. 13, 1954, p. 1, 7. Accessed Dec. 17, 2019. newspapers.com/image/56249688/.

"Flooded Rhode Island on Emergency Footing." *Hartford Courant*, Sept. 1, 1954, p. 8. Accessed Dec. 11, 2019. newspapers.com/image/371304788/?terms=Hurricane%2BCarol%2BConnecticut.

"Hurricane Death List 49, Loss Over 300 Million." *North Adams Transcript*, Mass., Sept. 1, 1954, p. 1, 18. Accessed Dec. 12, 2019. newspapers.com/image/54771588/.

Landers, Carol. "Vineyard Snugs Down for Storm." *Boston Globe*, Sept. 11, 1954, p. 10. Accessed Dec. 12, 2019. newspapers.com/image/433376569/?terms=Hurricane%2BEdna.

"Maine Termed Disaster Area by President." *Lewiston Daily Sun*, Sept. 14, 1954, p. 1, 9. Accessed Dec. 13, 2019. google.com/newspapers?id=o0MpAAAAIBAJ&sjid=zWYFAAAAIBAJ&dq=hurricane%20edna&pg=6542%2C4925077.

"New Haven Fights to Reopen Line." *Hartford Courant*, Sept. 1, 1954, p. 8. Accessed Dec. 11, 2019. newspapers.com/image/371304788/?terms=Hurricane%2BCarol%2BConnecticut.

"Norwich Hit Hard As Six Are Injured." *Hartford Courant*, Sept. 1, 1954, p. 8. Accessed Dec. 11, 2019. newspapers.com/image/371304788/?terms=Hurricane%2BCarol%2BConnecticut.

"Property Losses Soar; Disaster Areas Declared." *Bridgeport Telegram*, Sept. 1, 1954, p. 1. Accessed Dec. 11, 2019. newspapers.com/image/23028099/.

"Rhode Island." *Boston Globe*, Sept. 11, 1954, p. 10. Accessed Dec. 12, 2019. newspapers.com/image/433376569/?terms=Hurricane%2BEdna.

Rhodes, C. E. "North Atlantic Hurricanes and Tropical Disturbances-1954." US Weather Bureau, *National Atmospheric Administration, National Environmental Satellite, Data, and Information Service, National Climatic Center*, 1955, pp. 72–73. Accessed Dec. 13, 2019. books.google.com/books?id=hxPOAAAAMAAJ&pg=PA72&dq=hurricane+edna+1954&hl=en&sa=

X&ei=xIH0UNmVBMfF0QHMjoDgAQ&ved=0CFAQ6AEwBg#v=
onepage&q=hurricane%20edna%201954&f=false.

Sebestyen, Jules. "Fairfield Families Evacuate Flooded Dwellings at Beach."
*Bridgeport Telegram*, Sept. 1, 1954, p. 9. Accessed Dec. 11, 2019. news
papers.com/image/23028299/.

"Tents Struck as Hurricane Menaces Shows." *Boston Globe*, Sept. 11, 1954, p.
10. Accessed Dec. 12, 2019. newspapers.com/image/433376569/?terms=
Hurricane%2BEdna.

Ward, Bob. "Milford Orders Emergency Steps." *Bridgeport Telegram*, Sept. 1,
1954, p. 9. Accessed Dec. 11, 2019. newspapers.com/image/23028299/.

Ward, Robert F. "Damage Survey Under Way in Storm-Battered Milford."
*Bridgeport Telegram*, Sept. 1, 1954, p. 10. Accessed Dec. 11, 2019. news
papers.com/image/23028324/.

"Westbrook Woman and Child Saved." *Hartford Courant*, Sept. 1, 1954, p.
8. Accessed Dec. 11, 2019. newspapers.com/image/371304788/?terms=
Hurricane%2BCarol%2BConnecticut.

"Worcester Man Blown 10 Stories to Death." *Hartford Courant*, Sept. 1,
1954, p. 8. Accessed Dec. 11, 2019. newspapers.com/image/371304788/
?terms=Hurricane%2BCarol%2BConnecticut.